BROKEN
WORKS
BEST

By the same author:
God Knows Your Name
Under the Rainbow
Rainbows for Rainy Days
When We Can't, God Can
Chasing the Dawn

Catherine Campbell

BROKEN WORKS BEST

When God Turns Your Pain into Gain

10 Publishing
a division of 10ofthose.com

Dedicated to the brave children of Mae La Mu

Contents

Prologue   9

ONE:
BE PREPARED
Pain – part of the package   19
Why me? Investigating the cause   29
Why me? Persecution – the suffering we choose   37
Forward planning   45

TWO:
GAINING PERSPECTIVE
Seeing through different eyes   53
Comparisons – avoiding the pitfalls   61
How big is God?   67
God in pain   79

THREE:
DOES GOD CARE?
How does God see me?   87
The question of fairness   97
When angels come to call   107
Do I care?   121

FOUR:
LOOKING AFTER YOUR SOUL
Weeding – dealing with bitterness   129
Planting – what is good   137
Cultivating prayer – the upward look   147
Forgiving – a journey worth making   155

FIVE:
REAPING THE RESULTS

Don't waste your pain   169
The gospel will prosper   177
Broken works best   187
Heaven – the ultimate gain   201
A note from the author   215

Prologue

I am a coward, and not embarrassed to say so.

Heights terrify me, the sight of a mouse will send me running, but roller coasters take me beyond the pale. They are something else. They make my blood run cold.

The worldwide appeal of being pulled up steep iron tracks in a small metal car, high above the ground, only to be suddenly and violently hurled in the opposite direction, whilst whizzing around sharp bends, escapes me. The dichotomy of squealing in terror one minute and yelling with obvious delight the next during the two-minute thrill-ride consistently puzzles me, and is at odds with my longing for a safe existence.

Yet the term "roller coaster" had not been mentioned when I slipped into the back seat of a 4x4 truck a few hours earlier. As my head hit the ceiling one more time, I wondered if somehow a short theme-park ride would be almost preferable to my present journey. Still, at least we were in contact with the ground ... for the most part!

Catching the young Thai driver's bemused expression in the rear-view mirror, I realized that the moans, stifled groans and occasional squeals of three middle-aged ladies would undoubtedly fuel his conversation when he returned later that night to Mae Sariang.

Thankfully, it was the dry season.

On this occasion clouds of dust were preferable to the torrential rain and mudslides of the rainy season as we made our way along the mountain road to Mae La Mu. The tarmacadam road was by now many miles behind us, and our little convoy of four trucks continued along a mud track cut out of and around the mountainous terrain of the Thai–Burma border. The scenery was both fabulous and frightening as our vehicle came much too close to the cliff edge on more than one occasion. The tossing about in the cab provided a welcome diversion at times, shifting our concern from matters of safety to our ability to actually stay in our seats. Conversation was virtually at a standstill; we spoke in staccato snatches as we bumped over innumerable hard clay ridges.

"What on earth made the UN put this refugee camp so far from civilization?" I managed to verbalize during the relief of a few hundred yards of fairly flat road.

"Looks like they want to keep its location a secret." "Or … they want to make sure no one can escape from it."

Either response was probably not far from the truth. This was surely the long road to nowhere, leading to a bleak place on a troubled border that the rest of the world would rather forget.

"Remember, no photographs until we reach the orphanage! Keep your windows closed! No stopping on the way!"

The words chilled our excitement.

The trucks having been checked for "ghosts" (unregistered refugees), our little convoy was waved through the gate of Mae La Mu. And we entered an altogether different world.

The mud road through the refugee camp was narrow. The sights around us, harrowing.

No one spoke.

Wood-and-bamboo huts lined the road, inches apart. They all

looked the same – rickety, leaf-roofed homes, built on log stilts to let the flood waters of the rainy season run underneath to the river below. Thin interwoven bamboo strips provided walls of sorts – an attempt at privacy in this less-than-private world. Mangy chickens ran around little piles of wood, pecking at what, I didn't know; eating dirt in the absence of anything better. Skinny dogs were everywhere, while down at the river's edge a few men were making an attempt at fishing. But it was the dry season. The river water was very low, so their success would be limited. Indeed, their endeavours were virtually pointless.

And the bank on the other side of the river was Burma – home.

Home to these displaced people. So near and yet so far. Driven out by their own government; burnt out of their homes; tortured; tormented; starved; murdered. All because they are a tribal people – the Karen – and many of them Christian believers.

Yard after weary yard, we painstakingly made our way through the UN camp, which, built on the side of a mountain, housed 15,000 people. The road was barely wide enough to accommodate our 4x4. People had to step on to the rough clay verge to allow us through, and occasionally – just occasionally – my eyes would meet with those of a man or woman for whom Mae La Mu was their enforced home.

The glancing exchange revealed pain in the raw.

Looking into the eyes of the dejected ... the forsaken ... the hated ... the hopeless: recognizing that the disdain in those same eyes was directed towards us. These people don't want charity. They would rather grow their own rice; educate their own children; live in their own land; worship in freedom.

Trucks laden with food only serve to remind them of what they have become. Like the many foreigners who had come before us, we were trespassers in their dark world, needed but not welcome. The windows of the vehicle may have been tightly closed but the pervasive stench of hopelessness easily oozed in through the vents.

Unexpectedly the truck screeched to a halt, throwing us forward.

"Oh no," groaned my friend from the front seat, as we strained forward, trying to see the cause of her distress. "That dog's back legs are broken!"

The pathetic puppy was trying to drag its back end across the narrow road, while people simply ignored its existence, never mind its pain. No one cared – it was just a dog, after all. And as I watched the empty faces that fronted devastated lives, my heart cried: *"Everything's* broken here, Lord!"

The smiling faces of children and teenagers soon helped to lift our spirits as we finally exited our roller-coaster cab and walked up the long steep path to the orphanage. Their willing hands carrying bag after bag of supplies, they covered the rough terrain with ease, as sure-footed as mountain goats. Happy chatter replaced silent stares. Laughing echoed along the path. It was hard to believe we were still in the same place. And for a short time the atmosphere matched the bright sunshine of a truly beautiful day.

"How old are you?"

"Do you have a brother?"

"How many children do you have?"

We were perfect fodder for practising English conversation, the one vital school subject that might just lead to a work permit from the Thai authorities – a ticket out of this prison without parole. They came as children seeking safety; now, young adults, they were trapped, unwanted by the countries that flanked their jungle home.

In return they answered our questions.

"My father died when our village was attacked."

"My mother died in the jungle when we were trying to escape."

"My little sister died of malaria because we had no medicine."

"I lost my leg when I stood on a landmine."

And the smiles briefly slipped from the faces of these children, who had seen things that should be alien to the young; who had experienced heartache of cataclysmic proportions. My eyes scanned the edge of the group to the quiet sufferers – those who, as yet, had been unable to put their horrors into words, hiding dreadful secrets in their hearts.

Knowing what we did made it difficult to teach the Bible memory verse we had chosen for our visit. Our little team felt such heartache in sharing words that were such a vital reality for these children: easily spoken in the West, but deeply felt amongst these damaged young lives. Yet their loud, strong voices echoed back words written by the prophet Isaiah many centuries earlier, bringing us the comfort that we had hoped to deliver to them: "Don't be afraid, for I am with you. Don't lose hope, for I am your God. I will make you strong and help you" (Isaiah 41:10 NLT, adapted).

As I looked into the beautiful faces of 171 children, my resolve began to waver. Old questions that I thought I had laid to rest years earlier began to surface, as I heard myself question God on their hopeless plight. And then, as if to condemn my doubting thoughts, they began to sing – singing such as I had never heard before. Faces heavenward; hands raised or clutched to their chests; voices raised in unashamed praise of their wonderful Saviour. A sound that undoubtedly reached the throne-room of Heaven as a sweet-smelling sacrifice of praise, bringing joy to the Father's heart. Guilt mixed easily with my sorrow as I recognized an old Gaither tune I knew so well, now sung by some of the bravest people I have ever met:

Because He lives I can face tomorrow,
Because He lives all fear is gone,
Because I know, I know who holds the future.
And life is worth the living just because He lives.

Extract taken from the song "Because He Lives" by William & Gloria Gaither. Copyright © 1971 Gaither Music Company/ Thankyou Music

And I wept.

Silence once more filled the cab of the silver truck as we slowly made our way back through the camp towards the manned gate. Each of us was busy with our own thoughts of the children and young people we had met, of the horrendous stories we had been told. Why did it have to be this way? It was all so unfair; cruel, even. All around us I could sense the darkness of despair once more. Women and children in their thousands, with so few men, each burdened with a heavy sorrow I could do nothing about. The orphanage was different to the rest of this oppressed place. Somehow, at the back of this dark world, perched on a rocky hill, was a place of joy, laughter – and even hope.

A smile crossed my face as God planted a comforting thought in my mixed-up emotions:

Their singing doesn't only reach Heaven, Catherine. They are my "city set on a hill, that cannot be hidden". They are the light in this dark world. (Matthew 5:14, paraphrase.)

As I watched the people turn their heads away as we drove past, I realized that strangers cannot reach the hearts of these broken people. But the songs of other broken people, reaching down through that miserable place day after day, could.

They are not forgotten by God. Instead, He makes His presence felt and His love known through the lives of 171 children every day in Mae La Mu.

Prologue

The big gate clunked shut behind us. Our young driver turned the key in the ignition as I grabbed the steadying strap hanging above me. In a cloud of dust we were off, and as my nose pressed against the glass I whispered: "Broken definitely works best here, Lord."

ONE

BE PREPARED

Pain – part of the package

I don't know what it is about a newborn baby that captures your heart so completely.

Perhaps it's the sight of perfection in miniature: the tiny toes and fingers; the wrinkled skin that looks almost too big for such a small frame, while feeling softer than the exquisite work of the rarest silkworm. Or maybe it's the unrepeatable expressions that cross her beautiful face as she sleeps; the smell of baby powder; her utter dependence on you for her every need. I just don't know.

I only know that, from the first day we set eyes on her, our firstborn stole my heart, as well as that of her proud daddy. Beautiful, blue-eyed and blonde, she wrapped her little life tighter around ours with each passing day.

Then, barely seven months later, words spoken by a paediatrician swept over us like a tornado. Wreaking havoc, they turned our hitherto ordered lives upside down. Those words branded our child, destroyed our plans, devastated our family, clouded our future, and broke our hearts.

"Mrs Campbell," he said, "don't you realize your little girl is handicapped? She will never be normal."

The anguish of soul that followed such a damning diagnosis catapulted my life into a very dark place of pain, confusion, disbelief and despair.

The tragedies of life have a way of doing that, don't they? One minute life is wonderful, and the next, everything is falling apart. What was previously sure and certain suddenly falters. The present melts into a chaotic state; the future no longer holds what you had planned.

Survival, at some level, becomes the daily challenge.

Even simple physical chores seem insurmountable. Decision-making is often one step too far. And tears, anger and denial are constantly battling for prime position in an already cluttered mind; to say nothing of the pain – that constant tormenter of the life you never thought would be yours.

And none of it makes any sense.

Especially for those who know God as our Father, Jesus as our Saviour and the Holy Spirit as our teacher.

What went so terribly wrong here? What happened to Fatherly protection? Why did God not come up with the goods when I needed Him? Where was the promised happy life now? Have I been struck down, struck out, judged, condemned, forgotten or, worse still, ignored?

Heartache wasn't part of the deal.

The deal was that I give up my sin and become a follower of Jesus. Jesus lives in me through the presence of His Holy Spirit, and His forgiveness, love and peace give me the life I have always dreamed of. A joy-filled, purpose-driven, exciting life of walking with God. He could have everything; my life, my career and my home were dedicated to Him. That was what I had signed up to, willingly and wholeheartedly.

I loved Him.

He already had all of me.

Why did He have to break my heart?

It's funny how we think we have life all worked out. Every single area of our lives is organized and filed away in such neat little compartments. Family, work, home, friends, church; each of the portions that make up who we are is divided into manageable pieces. Pieces that, when working in harmony, produce a pleasant carefree world for us both to enjoy and feel productive in.

Life, however, is never quite that simple. In fact, the life we are called to live in Jesus is alien to the one we would normally choose. The only problem is, few of us have read the small print.

Suffering, pain and heartache become the magnifying glass that lets us see what this life with Jesus is really all about.

We ignore the small print at our peril!

For when one of our "essentials for a happy life" starts showing cracks, or worse still, violently implodes, we discover the package doesn't contain what we thought. There is more in there than we bargained for.

Or perhaps it should not have come as such a surprise. Could it be that we were only interested in the "good" bits? The truth was not, in fact, hidden. Heartache is out there; suffering wrecks lives. We simply prefer to believe that God wouldn't let it happen to us.

What would we think of a construction engineer in Christchurch, New Zealand, who ignored the tectonic fault line running under the country, because "it might never happen"? How would we feel if he built homes unable to withstand the force of an earthquake because the sun usually shines in New Zealand? How would we judge his professionalism, his ethics, his humanity, if one day the earth shook and rubble was all that was left? We would, of course, be horrified and would be baying for his blood!

Yet, as Christians we frequently make that mistake.

We ignore the fault line we all live on – the fault line of pain, suffering and heartache that underlies each one of our lives. We lull ourselves into a false sense of security, thinking that "It will never happen to me", and making no preparation should disaster strike one day.

I know. For that is exactly what happened in my life.

I never dreamed I would ever be the recipient of such horrific news from a paediatrician. As far as I was concerned, I had done everything right. Humanly speaking, I was fit and healthy; I ate all the right foods; I didn't smoke or abuse alcohol or drugs. There was no obvious medical indicator that the child I was carrying was anything but normal. I was simply excited, happy and looking forward to becoming a mum for the first time. And because I was a Christian I thought the little bundle tucked away inside me had the automatic right to the protection of God – and to perfection.

My unconscious reasoning was that I loved God and therefore He would never let anything really bad happen to me, or to those I loved. After all, I wasn't only a Christian – I was married to a preacher! My husband was one of God's servants. And up until that point, our plans were to serve God overseas. We were prepared to give up everything, cross the world and devote our lives to whatever God had planned for us. Surely that was even more reason for God to protect our lives from the disasters we had seen in the lives of others?

In spite of my knowledge of the Bible; in spite of the privilege of godly teaching in my home church; in spite of all I had seen as a nurse in Belfast's troubled times, my theology was deeply flawed. I genuinely never believed any of the "big stuff" would fall on me.

I had ignored the fault line I was sitting on.

And in one short afternoon my world fell apart.

Those words, "never be normal", tormented my every waking moment. The future for our little daughter was bleak beyond imagination and the dreams we had for our own lives lay in tatters. And right in the middle of this disaster, the wind of confusion rocked my trust in a God who had been in control of my life since I was fourteen years old. Surely He could have nothing to do with this? Surely something so monstrous must have come from the pit? My questions loomed larger than the paltry little pile of answers that didn't seem to hold water any more. Platitudes I had given to others were simply that – platitudes.

And the persistent assault of Scripture verses that friends wanted to leave with me, to soothe my sorrow, only added to the torment I was experiencing. It approached something similar to a spiritual firing squad. Rather than give me confidence, the words of Romans 8:28 – "All things work together for good to those who love God, to those who are the called according to His purpose" – seared my heart. How could anything good ever come from this? What did the deliverers of those words know about how I was feeling? What gave them the right to quote Scripture at me?

After-shocks can come in many guises – anger, disbelief, intense disappointment, deep sadness, and a weariness of body and soul. All are then fuelled by our spiritual enemy, adding insult to the injury already caused by another source.

In my case the resultant damage was constant, unremitting heartache. I tried so hard to display a smile when I went to church. After all, it was expected of me. Christians are not meant to question! Quiet acceptance is supposed to be the norm. And when I caught the odd whisper of "Isn't she doing well? If anyone can get through it, they can," I thought my secret was safe. No one else need know of the questioning spirit that had replaced the strong confidence I previously held in God.

Thankfully, a disaster management plan had already been set in motion. God was on my case, help was on the way, and the process of reaching my heart had begun.

Each one of us is very different. There are those who have no problem in treading the path of faithful trust, for whom a questioning heart is unthinkable. They are already totally aware of the frailty of life, and their response when suffering touches them is: "Why not? I am no different to anyone else." They therefore have less rubble to clear before God's healing begins to reach them. After many years, my response to heartache has had a gargantuan shift. Unfortunately it has taken me a long time to reach where I am now. Yet the learning has taken me to places with God that I never dreamed possible.

For the majority of us, questions abound when disaster hits our lives. We tend to think, respond and act in multifarious ways, especially when under stress. Yet God's rescue plans are much more simple, whatever our make-up, whatever our response. That is because His endgame is always the same – to get us to the place of acceptance. As Amy Carmichael discovered so long ago: "In acceptance lieth peace."

While we wonder what to do next, our heavenly Father knows the three basic elements we need to begin our healing. We need to be aware of His presence – to know that we are not alone; to be reminded of His love – reassuring us of His care over us; and to hear Him speak into our pain – communicating with us in our sorrow. And while the unwise use of Scripture in the hands of the well-meaning can at times cause pain, the converse is true when God Himself whispers His word to our hearts. It has true healing power.

When these three elements begin to come together, the rubble of anger, disbelief and disappointment can start to be removed, allowing His love room to once more reach our hearts.

With me, the gentle excavation began one evening when I was alone in our bedroom. Cheryl was fast asleep and my husband, Philip, was away preaching. Hiding under the duvet had become my safe place to end each day. Away from the gaze of others, I could cry, pray, and plead alone. Here, in my bedding tent, the mask that I hid behind during daylight hours could be dropped. That evening was no different. Wet pillows and quilted covers swallowed up the same pleading words I uttered every night:

"Lord, You can make Cheryl well – I know You can. Why does it have to be this way? It doesn't make any sense. Help me, because I don't know what You are doing in my life!"

The only difference that night, from the many that had preceded it, was that God responded in an amazing way, speaking to my broken heart. My despair was interrupted by a wonderful sense that God had crept into the room. I lay, still covered by the duvet, listening to the powerful silence, yet experiencing the tangible presence of my heavenly Father in a way I never had before. Peace filled each crevice, not only of the room, but also of my heart.

"You were there all the time," were the words that formed in my mind, yet remained unspoken.

Such was the feeling of His presence that I couldn't speak, and I was afraid that if I pulled the covers back I would see Him. So I stayed where I was, thrilled that I had not been abandoned by the One who had meant so much to me, up until this point in my life.

And then I heard Him speak.

The moment was surreal and yet more real than anything I had ever experienced before: a strange mixture of the unbelievable and the tangible combining to become reality.

The words that God used originated in my own heart, echoing in my mind, and drawn from my memory, reminding me of something that I had read in the Bible years earlier. They were not the booming of a supernatural voice, but rather a quiet reminder of the message God had given to His prophet Isaiah many years ago:

But now, thus says the LORD, who created you, O Jacob,
And He who formed you, O Israel:
"Fear not, for I have redeemed you;
I have called you by your name;
You are Mine.
When you pass through the waters, I will be with you;

And through the rivers, they shall not overflow you.
When you walk through the fire, you shall not be burned,
Nor shall the flame scorch you.
*For I am the L*ORD *your God,*
The Holy One of Israel, your Saviour.

ISAIAH 43:1–3A

In an instant – a divine moment in time – my rescue had begun.

The overwhelming reality of God's peace calmed every ounce of my being. As I allowed the words to wash over me from head to foot, inside and out, I knew with absolute certainty that the promise of God's presence was mine – whatever lay ahead. He had created me, formed me and even knew my name. Those truths made my heart do somersaults! I was His child; He was my Saviour. And He would never leave me to face this disaster alone.

Sweet, restful sleep followed quickly for the first time in weeks.

The following morning, with great excitement I flicked over the pages of my Bible to find the words that God had whispered to my heart the previous night. I wanted to look more closely at all that God was saying. The shifting of the rubble around my life would require more than a peaceful night's rest, however good that felt. The assurance that God was already actively involved in my rescue spurred me on.

I knew He had more to say.

Like many Christians, I was in the habit of reading a portion of the Bible every day. God is a speaking God, and He has chosen to use His written Word, the Bible, as His principal way of communicating with His children. It is, however, easy to get into a routine with Bible reading. You do it like you do your teeth; a daily habit. When you read something encouraging, it tends to give you a lift for the day. When you are trudging your way through the hard passages, you are glad to get to the end, somehow or other convincing yourself that they need to be there, but not for you.

A bit like "Pick-n-Mix", we choose the bits that bring us most enjoyment and leave the rest for someone else to pick up.

The opening verses of Isaiah 43 are a lot like that.

I recalled reading these verses as a young teenager. Their immediate impact had a "Wow!" factor. The only problem was that I had subconsciously ignored at least 50 per cent of the biblical teaching in the verse. These truths are of such importance that, had I embraced them as a teenager, it would have much better prepared me for that fateful day when my underlying fault line shifted and disaster hit our home.

It was the word "when" in the passage that was the give-away to my earlier folly. For some unknown reason I had substituted it with the word "if", making the whole three verses much more palatable, yet rendering them useless as any form of preparation for real life.

Verse 2 said, *when* you pass through the waters of difficulty, not *if; when* you go through rivers of disappointment, not *if; when* you walk through the fire of suffering, not *if*. The clear use of the word "when" was every bit as much an absolute as the promise that accompanied it: "I will be with you."

Through the prophet Isaiah God was telling His children that there were hard, if not disastrous times ahead. That was a definite – not merely a maybe.

The book of Job has a similar message.

This man, whom God described as "the finest man in all the earth … a man of complete integrity" (Job 1:8 NLT), had plenty to say about suffering after losing seven sons and three daughters in one day, to say nothing of his livestock and property. Job exclaimed: "Man who is born of woman is of few days and full of trouble" (Job 14:1).

A short life full of trouble is all we can expect, was Job's assessment of our lives. Gloomy stuff that you might expect from someone who had it so tough. But the same message is repeated over and over again in Scripture.

Moving into the New Testament, the words of Jesus Himself reinforce what we would rather avoid: "He makes His sun rise on the evil and on the good, and sends rain on the just and on the unjust" (Matthew 5:45). The rain falls on us all, and there is no spiritual umbrella for the Christian. God treats us all the same. He has no favourites. It is as straightforward as this.

Pain is part of the package.

In spite of what, on the surface, appears to be an announcement of doom and gloom, some kind of dark prophecy of looming disaster, the truth behind this bleak revelation is surprisingly comforting.

If pain is simply part and parcel of what it means to be human, then it also means that I have not been singled out for disaster. God is not some malevolent spiritual being meting out harm on His subjects. Quite the opposite, in fact, as He promises His presence with us through whatever this fallen world throws at us.

Rather than pronouncing impending misery, the Bible is God's early warning system to help us limit the damage when our fault lines begin to shake. The "It'll never happen to me" approach will only add to the rubble that needs to be cleared when the unthinkable happens in our lives.

How much better it is to be prepared, to accept that pain is part of the package – not with fatalistic negativism, but with the full knowledge that when the storm hits, God is ready to put His master disaster plan into action on our behalf.

Why me? Investigating the cause

My husband is a pastor; therefore we live in the church manse.

It can be a bit like "living above the shop". There are no office hours, either with the job, or with our home. Our home phone number is also the church contact number; hence we are on call twenty-four hours a day. When the phone rings before 8 a.m. it is more than likely that one of the local funeral directors is calling to say that someone from our congregation has died during the night.

Being wakened in the middle of the night by the piercing ringing of the phone is something you never get used to. For a few seconds a feeling of dread grips you as you try to put your brain into gear before lifting the receiver. Is it church? Is it family? Whatever the origin of the call, you are certain that what you are about to hear is bad news. Disaster, however, has no favourite time of day; it can come just as easily in daylight hours as in the shadows of the night.

"I'm sorry to bother you," is often how the conversation starts, "but my husband has had a massive heart attack … my nephew reversed over his little boy with the tractor … the news from the hospital is bad – it's cancer … my grandson's body has just been pulled out of the river … the transplant team have arrived; the family would like you to be here with them … my son-in-law has attempted to murder my daughter!"

Broken Works Best

Life-taking and life-threatening situations always cause the silent groan of sympathy to be mixed with a feeling of inadequacy as you seek to respond immediately to the most urgent of calls. And, *no*, you never get used to being early on the scene of personal tragedy. To walk into the lives of those experiencing the searing pain of heartache at its height is always so very difficult. Our calling as Christians is to "Bear one another's burdens, and so fulfil the law of Christ" (Galatians 6:2), but those in pastoral ministry work at the rock-face with their feet firmly placed amongst the broken pieces. And it is not pretty.

On the other side of the pain-coin are marital breakdowns, abandonment, teen pregnancy, business collapse, chronic illness, mental health issues … and the list goes on. These devastating situations of life may not hit the headlines, but they have at their heart individuals – individuals in pain.

And once the dust settles, the next stage is a longing to try to make sense of what seems so senseless, a desire or a deep-felt need to blame something or someone for shattered lives. If a reason could be found then, perhaps, the pain would be easier to bear, and reconstruction of what remains might appear to be possible.

Tucked amongst the questions that inevitably arise is the hardest question of all. Some are bold enough or angry enough to speak the word, whilst others allow it to fester in secret, afraid that uttering it might add to their heartache or call their faith into doubt.

"WHY?"

"Why has this happened to *me*?" And the progression continues.

"Why? Why did God allow this to happen?"

And disappointment is added to the mix.

"Why? Why did God not stop this from happening?"

And anger and confusion expand the cracks in our broken hearts.

"Why? Why doesn't God step in and do something *now*?"

"Why?"

"Why?" is such a tiny word. Only three letters long, yet it holds such power over us. It attacks our reason; causes us to doubt; confuses our beliefs; leaves us feeling guilty and, worst of all, it is a question that is rarely answered to our satisfaction, especially when it relates to personal pain.

Adam and Eve certainly have a lot to answer for.

It had all started so well for them. No one would ever again enjoy the privileges this couple experienced. They had been created in perfection; they lived in the most beautiful natural surroundings; their needs were provided for; they had work to occupy their days and the presence of the God of Heaven walking with them in the garden in the cool of the evening. As man and wife they complemented each other so well. Their lives were safe and secure: perfect in every way.

Until one day Eve looked where she shouldn't have looked, and listened to the serpent's sly words, causing her to doubt God's command to her husband: "but of the tree of the knowledge of good and evil you shall not eat" (Genesis 2:17). Enticed by ambition and blinded by lies, Eve desired what was not hers to have and took what God had forbidden.

Adam, standing close by, in a display of weakness and abandonment of his God-given leadership, accepted the offered fruit from his wife. From that single act of defiant disobedience their world, and ours, was changed forever.

Sin had dreadful consequences for Adam and Eve.

Their perfect world was overrun by thistles and thorns; pain and sickness, even murder and mayhem would be their legacy. The privilege of partnering with the Creator in producing children would now be spoilt by the pain that would forever be associated with childbirth. Homeless and bereft, Adam and Eve were expelled from their paradise home to fend for themselves in an unknown and hostile environment.

Centuries later, the apostle Paul was to pen: "Therefore, just as through one man sin entered the world, and death through sin, and thus death spread to all men, because all sinned ..." (Romans 5:12).

You see, the dreadful consequences of sin were not confined to Adam and Eve. Because we now live in a world damaged by the fall, a world that is not as it was intended to be, we all suffer with pain as part of the natural order.

Sickness was not God's plan; heartache was not meant to be; death was not His intention for us, but rather, His desire was for us to have life – in perfection. But sin spoilt the master plan.

Since those Eden days, sin has been inextricably linked with pain and the resultant suffering of mankind. This is the answer to the question of why suffering is caused by the natural order. We don't choose it. It comes along with bodies and societies that are afflicted with the consequences of original sin.

This generalized answer to "Why?" covers the big picture to a degree, but as individuals we are more concerned with the "me" part of the "Why me?" question. It's a minority view, but there are those who equate *all* personal suffering with personal sin. Find the sin, they argue, and you'll be free of the suffering, once you repent.

As a family we were once the targets of such theological folly. Shortly after being told of Cheryl's diagnosis, we received a letter challenging us to get on our knees before God in order to identify the sin that had apparently caused our daughter's disability. We were told in no uncertain terms that our repentance was vital if we were to see her healed.

Already in an emotionally devastating place, the letter upset me deeply, causing me to wonder if indeed Cheryl's condition was our fault. After prayer and a look at the Bible together, my husband and I were able to consign that letter to the "unwise advice" box in our lives. However, it took longer for me to recover spiritually from the anger and bitterness that remained following such thoughtless action, however well meant at the time.

It has to be said that some sinful practices undoubtedly do lead to illness, personal pain and family anguish, as with alcohol and drug abuse, sexual promiscuity and crime, but there is no biblical basis for the idea that each person's pain is fallout from some specific sin.

Jesus made that very clear in John 9:1–3, when He was asked *whose* sin was the cause of a man's blindness. In reply He assured the gathered crowd that neither the man nor his parents were responsible for the condition that rendered him blind from birth. Instead Jesus pointed them to the fact that the man's life circumstances were about more than his lack of sight, but rather, "that the works of God should be revealed in him" (verse 3). The man's disability was not associated with personal sin. His personal suffering was part of a much bigger picture, and the same is true for all of us.

Some may think that we take the easy way out when we blame the curse of a fallen world for the pain and personal suffering that afflicts us all at some time or another. Not so, because it then leads to the next question, which is one we would prefer to avoid: Where does God fit into all of this?

How do we deal with the "Why didn't God …?" or "Why did God …?" questions that abound?

"Why didn't God stop that accident from happening?"

"Why did God allow my mum to develop cancer?"

"Why did God take my two daughters from me?"

"Why does God stand by while those little children in Africa starve?"

The answer to these and many other questions is found in the sovereignty of God. Yet the doctrine of the sovereignty of God can be both the most comforting and the most confusing of all spiritual teachings. We have no problem believing that God is in total control of our lives and our universe when everything is well with our little world. But when that fault line shakes and disaster strikes, the very truth that always made us feel secure can, conversely, make us feel vulnerable.

For me, the discovery that pain was part of the package in my life was much easier to accept than the minutiae of detail that surrounded our daughter's diagnosis. Did "she will never be normal" have to include epilepsy, curvature of the spine, inability to walk and a myriad of other disabilities that developed as the years went on? Surely God could have stepped in and stopped the process at the learning difficulty stage? Why did it have to get so bad?

Slowly, over a period of time, with God's gentle workings in my heart, I came to realize that the knowledge of a God in complete control, who makes no mistakes, and whose desire is always and only for our good, brings great comfort in times of heartache. The view that our suffering is a result of chaos, without the hand of God anywhere in the mix, is as disturbing as it is destructive.

Was my daughter simply a collection of damaged genes that rendered her profoundly disabled? As far as her disease was concerned, it was undoubtedly a result of the fall of man – part of the natural order. But as an individual, who was more than a physical being contracted to a time span, Cheryl had the stamp of God's eternal plan on her life. What was going on was about more than her, just like the blind man in John chapter 9.

So, does God *send* suffering or does He merely *allow* it?

The theologians have been working on this particular debate for centuries. I am not an academic, but in my study of God's

Word I try to work on a simple principle: *Don't allow what you don't understand about God to destroy what you already know about Him.*

Read in a contextual vacuum, Psalm 135:6 – "Whatever the LORD pleases He does, In heaven and in earth, In the seas and in all deep places" – paints God as unconcerned about the results of His actions. After all, "He can do what He likes"! Yet "Whatever the LORD pleases He does" cannot be separated from His divine character. The more we learn about His character, the more we realize that what God does in His sovereignty is always tied up in who He is.

Therefore, the God who numbers the very hairs on our head (Matthew 10:30) and collects our tears in a bottle (Psalm 56:8), the God "who did not spare his own Son, but gave him up for us all" (Romans 8:32 NIV), is also the God of Psalm 135:6.

The difficulties we may experience in understanding the doctrine of the sovereignty of God in the light of human suffering are tempered by the knowledge and evidence of the divine character. Our God is loving, caring, holy and just. Because of who He is, we need not be afraid to trust Him – even with the things that we don't understand.

There is no doubt that pain, and its related suffering, are results of the fall; they are now part of the natural order. But we are also part of a much bigger picture where God is working out His sovereign plan.

The causes of our pain are so intertwined with the purposes of God's big plan for mankind that they cannot be separated. Individual strands of suffering, woven together with strands of God's providence and grace, together make a beautiful and useful pattern, in spite of the complexity of their source, or their effect on our lives.

What greater illustration is there than the cross, where the Son of God died, suffering such physical and mental torture, in order that the great plan of salvation could become reality?

Broken Works Best

At the cross our "whys?" are brought into perspective, and we find rest.

I lay my "whys?"
before Your Cross
in worship kneeling,
my mind too numb
for thought,
my heart beyond
all feeling:

And worshipping,
realize that I
in knowing You
don't need a "why?"

RUTH BELL GRAHAM[1]

Why me? Persecution – the suffering we choose

In this chapter names have been changed to protect the identities of those concerned, who still live and serve Christ in great danger.

Nanda jumped. Little beads of perspiration glistened on her forehead, her hand shaking slightly as she held a piece of cloth steadily against the run of the needle.

Another car door slammed and the laughter of loud male voices pierced through the fragile walls of the small building housing the sewing class. The pounding of Nanda's heart quietened as the sound of their footsteps faded. Breathing a sigh of relief, she wiped her brow, composing herself as another question came from the enthusiastic group of women gathered around her.

"My peace I give to you, Nanda."

The calming words distracted her briefly, washing over her like cool water on a hot day. Even in a room of chattering women, she found the voice of God so easy to hear, and her heart responded in a silent issue of praise. The God who had protected her before, would never abandon her.

Before …

On another day, in a similar situation, in a different village, she had heard the slamming of car doors, men laughing loudly.

On that day, as the door was pushed open, the women started screaming, quickly pulling the khimars over their heads, hiding terrified faces behind their veils.

At first Nanda was indignant that men should burst in, frightening the ladies of her sewing class, but before she could get to her feet to protest, she heard the words she had dreaded for so long:

"Christian dog!" they screamed at her, spitting, and reaching forward to grab her over the sewing machine that stood between them.

Mayhem ensued. Nanda could feel the skin on her shins tear as the metal edges of the machine dug deep, as her body was dragged over anything that blocked her assailants' path to the door. Out of the corner of her eye she saw the other women cowering, faces covered, as their precious sewing machines were smashed against the walls.

"Don't be afraid!" she heard herself call out to those dear women, as her bleeding feet were pulled across the door-frame.

"Is this the day, Lord? Is this the day I will die?" her heart whispered.

The men were too strong. Nanda couldn't free herself from their grip. She cried for help. In the street others scurried past, as her evil captors pushed and shoved her into a waiting car, Islam's fear-driven culture making cowards of those who passed by. There was no rescue for this twenty-year-old whose only crime was that of being a follower of Jesus Christ.

As she slipped into unconsciousness she could hear the words of her Saviour: "If they persecuted Me, they will also persecute you" (John 15:20).

This attack had come as no surprise to Nanda.

The days that followed were the stuff of nightmares. Having passed out in the car, Nanda had no idea how far she had come or where she was being held. Looking around her prison, she discovered it was no different from most of the houses that cluttered the villages throughout the war-torn Valley of Kashmir. Very little furniture, broken pots and an old two-ring gas camping stove took up space in a dingy, grey room. Except that in this room the windows were boarded up, physical darkness adding to the spiritual darkness that hung rancid in the air. A dirty, ragged rug covered part of the floor, but she was not allowed to sit on it. Instead her captors used it for *salat*, praying five times every day in the hope that they would achieve spiritual benefit and eventually eternal reward.

Five times every day Nanda would be forced to face the wall in the corner of the small room, hands tied tightly behind her back. Ten times in each *salat* she would hear the invocation begin with the words *"Allahu Akbar"* ("God is great"). These were words she was familiar with; she had heard them every day of her life. Her father's voice rang in her ears as the men prayed, her eyes misting as the picture of her brothers joining him in ritual washing and prayer movements filled her mind. They had seemed such little boys when they accompanied their father to the mosque for their first public prayers. *"Allahu Akbar,"* they would proudly repeat, even before they knew what it meant.

Yet, it was only as a teenager that Nanda came to discover how great God really was. Night after night she would sneak out of the house and go to a secret location where meetings were being held to explain the message of the Christian gospel. Everyone who attended knew they would be in danger if they were caught listening to what the Qur'an described as "apostate teaching". People were known to have "disappeared" if found with a copy of the Bible. Others had lost their lives for openly declaring that they had left the Muslim faith to become Christian.

Apostasy is not tolerated in Islam.

As the men would engage in *salat*, Nanda would recount to herself how great God is. He is great in creation, in holiness, in justice, in love. That final thought was the one that grabbed her each and every day; that gave her the strength to go on in her captivity. It was the truth that made it possible for her to refuse to recant – whatever those men did to her. "For God so loved the world that He gave His only begotten Son, that whoever believes in Him should not perish but have everlasting life" (John 3:16).

The love of Christ had won her heart. His suffering and sacrifice on her behalf captivated her being. It also helped her to make sense of the apostle Paul's words in his letter to the young, suffering church at Philippi: "For you have been given not only the privilege of trusting in Christ but also the privilege of suffering for him" (Philippians 1:29 NLT). Now she knew these words were also for her.

Wasn't that what the evangelist told her on the very night she repented of her sin and trusted in Christ as her Saviour and Lord?

So when her beautiful body felt the weight of vicious blows from bony hands or leather straps, she would guard her mind and heart by reciting Scripture, drawing strength from the promises of God:

"Who shall separate us from the love of Christ? Shall tribulation, or distress, or persecution, or famine, or nakedness, or peril, or sword? ... For I am persuaded that neither death nor life, nor angels nor principalities nor powers, nor things present nor things to come, nor height nor depth, nor any other created thing, shall be able to separate us from the love of God which is in Christ Jesus our Lord" (Romans 8:35, 38–39).

Days passed into weeks as Nanda's captors tried to force her to recant and revert to Islam. Occasionally, despair mingled with the threats and torture meted out by the men, who thought they had the right to do so in the name of Allah or Mohammed.

Often Nanda longed for home, her family and the women she loved to work with. Would anyone tell them about Jesus now that she was gone? Was it one of these women that she had poured her life into, who had given her up to these wicked men? She would never know.

The darkest time of all was when she lay in the dirt, used, abused and purity gone. They had taken everything from her – except Jesus. On that night she understood Paul's heartfelt desire to "be with Christ, which is far better", but then she remembered that he went on to say: "But ... it is better that I continue to live" (Philippians 1:24 NLT). "Someone needs to tell these people about Jesus," she reckoned, as she nursed her bruised body.

As her eyes grew accustomed to the darkness, she could make out the forms of those who had brutalized her and, as hot tears flowed down her cheeks once more, she could sense the presence of Another in the room, who said:

"My grace is sufficient for you, *Nanda*, for My strength is made perfect in weakness" (2 Corinthians 12:9, italics mine).

And she wept again, as the love of Jesus wrapped itself around her.

Veer couldn't believe his ears.

"Praise God! You're alive! Where are you?"

The questions tumbled out as the evangelist heard the voice of someone he was convinced was dead by now. It was eight weeks since Nanda had been abducted from the sewing project. All their endeavours to find her had failed. But many people across the world had prayed for her deliverance – and God had graciously answered!

She sounded very weak and afraid as she tried to speak to Veer. Her breathless message was garbled and staccato-like: "The men have left me! I have escaped! Can you help me? I don't know what to do!"

The next few hours were the longest Veer had ever spent, as he searched for Nanda, with only a few clues as to her whereabouts.

"Behind a corrugated tin shed, near the market, with a battered Coca-Cola sign on a nearby wall."

He tried not to look shocked at the sight before him when Nanda peeked out from her hiding place. A faint smile crossed her bruised face, as Veer's wife covered her in a blanket and held her in a close embrace.

"God is good," were the only words the older woman could manage as she gently helped the injured Nanda into the back of their ancient truck. Right now Veer and his wife could only imagine what this brave young woman had endured for the sake of her Master.

Wisdom dictated that silence was best as Veer's old car bumped over rubble-strewn roads. Nanda was glad. In time, speaking about her ordeal would be part of the healing process, but for now she just wanted to be taken as far away from "that place" as she could possibly be.

She got her wish.

Delhi, India, was to be Nanda's place of safety and recovery. Here she was loved and cared for by brothers and sisters in Christ, allowed to build up her strength in every way. For six difficult, but healing, months her body and soul were mended, not only by human hands but also by the One for whom she had chosen to suffer. She knew in the light, what God had reminded her of in the darkness – that indeed, nothing could separate her from the love of God in Christ Jesus.

As time passed Nanda began to long once again for her valley home, and for the work that God had given her to do with the women of Kashmir. These precious Muslim women, who were destined to spend the majority of their lives inside the confines of their own homes, could only be reached by other women. And those willing to take the risk were so few.

Going home wasn't a difficult decision for Nanda to make, neither was it one made out of duty or under duress. She simply placed her life into God's hands and lived every day with the promise of Jesus: "lo, I am with you always, even to the end of the age" (Matthew 28:20).

And as the women tidied up after their first sewing class, they looked at this beautiful young teacher with freedom in her eyes, and wondered: "What is it about her that makes her look so different?"

They would soon know.

Suffering as a disciple is inevitable in Nanda's world. In fact, her experience is the norm that Jesus explained when He said: "If anyone desires to come after Me, let him deny himself, and take up his cross, and follow Me" (Matthew 16:24).

Thousands of people throughout the world know that when they choose to follow Jesus Christ, they are also choosing the very real possibility of suffering for the decision they have made. They do not chase after suffering, but it is almost certainly a by-product of Christian discipleship in the culture in which they live.

Yet Matthew 16:24 was not just written for the unfortunate few. Jesus makes it clear that this is to be the benchmark of discipleship for "anyone" who chooses to follow Him.

Who knows when our comfort in the West will end; when we who name the name of Christ will have to choose suffering, just as Nanda and Veer do every day?

Forward planning

It had been a lovely evening.

I had spent it with a group of young women, sharing something of my personal story and teaching from the Bible under the title of "Making Sense out of Suffering". Those present had listened with interest and the conversation over supper was very positive.

As I packed up to leave the group's leader thanked me warmly for coming but her assessment of the evening stunned me somewhat.

"That was very interesting," she said, "but we are all at such a good time in our lives at the minute that what you said isn't so relevant for us now." Trying to cover her tracks a bit, she added, stammering, "But I'm sure *someone* found it useful."

Saddened, I quietly replied, "We should be careful not to waste these good times that God has given us."

She had missed the point.

While few of us doubt the wisdom of saving for holidays or for our children's education, or of planning for our retirement, the idea of making preparation should suffering touch our lives seems alien to us. Instead we bury our head in the sand and determine that such negativity merits no thought, unless and until suffering strikes. It's a school of thought I once belonged to.

I mean, how gloomy is that – to prepare for trials? They might never come our way! Perhaps the young woman in question regarded me as rather melodramatic – a merchant of doom and gloom. Yet the Bible is so textually vast on the subject of suffering and its inevitability in our lives that we would all do well to make some preparation. Not to wait fatalistically for our world to fall in around us, but rather to fine tune our lives in such a way that we more easily recognize God's bigger plan in the realities of life.

Jill Briscoe, speaking at a ladies' conference I attended, made a very pertinent point: "Don't wait until the Chaldeans are running all over your living-room before you seek God!" Urging those present to build up a strong faith in Christ, she pointed to the prophecy that Habakkuk had received from the Lord concerning the imminent invasion of Israel by the warring Chaldeans. The nation would be devastated, and while Habakkuk was initially horrified, his comfort came from the knowledge he had of God up until that point. God's presence with His servant during the devastation was never in any doubt, but because Habakkuk already had a close relationship with God, the personal and national suffering was easier to accept. The battle within Habakkuk's heart was won before disaster struck: the enabling peace was already present before the invasion began.

As with Habakkuk, our personal walk with God will affect how we deal with the hard times. In the event of personal tragedy, a close, living relationship with Jesus Christ undoubtedly makes the journey towards acceptance and peace much shorter. Yet the reality of ever busier lives and the stealth attack of materialism have contributed to the "boxing up" of our Christian lives. We try to get by with the little commitment-packages of once on a Sunday and whatever else we can squeeze in through the week, but the process leaves us sluggish and ill prepared for the enemy camping on our borders.

And before we know it, the Chaldeans are running around our living-room! And we don't know how to respond.

So what is our walk with God really like? Perhaps a little reality check is in order.

How well do I know God? How much do I know of His character, His Word, His plan for my life – that I didn't know, say, five years ago? Am I merely a good sermon-taster – or am I seeking to get to know God for myself through regular personal study of the Bible? If my Bible were taken from me, as with Nanda, how much of it have I hidden in my heart so that it could continue to minister to me?

Can we withstand the annoyances of everyday life, the disappointments of friends, the unexpected sickness, the family crisis – without major spiritual fallout, because we already know who God is?

The truth of the matter is that none of us know exactly what is around the corner as far as health, wealth, employment and family are concerned. And consequently, we cannot prepare specifically for those things about which we have no knowledge. But we can spend our good times, when our heads are clear and our health is good, in developing the relationship God longs to have with us. And the amazing spin-off of this, delighting in God, will be preparation of soul and mind for whatever lies ahead.

However, some people are already standing in the rubble: preparation time is no longer available. The thing we thought would never happen, already has – and "if only" is pointlessly destructive. What is urgently needed is to experience personally the God who is "a very present help" in times of trouble (Psalm 46:1). For it is never too late to get close to Him: His desire is always towards us.

Listen to the heart of Jesus as He speaks in Matthew 11:28–29: "Come to Me, all you who labour and are heavy laden, and I will give you rest. Take My yoke upon you and learn from Me, for I am gentle and lowly in heart, and you will find rest for your souls."

Jesus offers to be our burden-bearer and rest-giver right in the middle of whatever weighs us down. His invitation also extends to those who still know little or nothing about Him: "all" marks the inclusiveness of God's desire to reach into shattered lives. We simply have to "come".

From that point of trust Jesus then offers to be our mentor as He encourages us to learn from Him: to be linked *together* with Christ through the difficulties of life. This is the promise of companionship instead of loneliness in our sorrow: the opportunity to learn how to handle the darkness with the One described as "a man of sorrows, acquainted with deepest grief" (Isaiah 53:3 NLT).

Surely history has testified to the many lives and situations that have been transformed by lessons learnt in the fiercest of human tragedies. Some, having recognized the inevitability of suffering before their fault line shook, are perhaps prepared to face the pain with more organized spiritual order, God's reassuring peace already battling the onslaught. Others, simply reaching out in the utter shock of devastation that has taken them by surprise, have discovered that God is still there for them too, reaching for them through the rubble with His gracious hand outstretched.

Notes
1. Ruth Bell Graham, *It's My Turn*, Hodder & Stoughton, 1982, p. 169.

Taking a closer look

- Examine the inevitability of suffering for yourself. Start with Job 14:1; Matthew 5:45; Isaiah 43:1–3a.

- Read Genesis 3 slowly and carefully note the seriousness and consequences of sin. Can you find the first mention of the Redeemer in this passage?

- The two causes of suffering – the natural order and persecution – are only part of God's bigger picture. List what you know of God's character that is always displayed in His sovereignty. Start with:

  God is Holy – Isaiah 6:3; Habakkuk 1:13a God is Love – John 3:16; 1 John 4:8

  God is Faithful – Lamentations 3:22–23

  Why not use a concordance to help you discover more?

- What are some of God's purposes when a believer suffers persecution? Look at these passages: Job 23:10; 2 Corinthians 12:9–10; Philippians 1:12–14; 2 Corinthians 4:16–18.

- Write down one thing that God has taught you in the past six months. Can you recite one Bible verse from memory? Is it possible for you to make a fair assessment of your present relationship with God?

- Read Isaiah 53 to remind yourself of who it is who wants to mentor us through the hard times.

TWO

GAINING
PERSPECTIVE

Seeing through different eyes

The aircraft's approach into Belfast City Airport that day was at a lower altitude than I had ever experienced before. Perhaps the pilot was enjoying the spectacular view along with the rest of us!

The Ards Peninsula looked resplendent as it pushed out into the Irish Sea, its attachment to the Irish mainland looking decidedly tenuous from this viewpoint. Suddenly I recognized my friend's house – a large, rambling old manse, clearly visible below me, in a pretty seaside village. In the short time it took for the plane to pass overhead, I was amazed at how different it all looked from this perspective. Places that I recognized not only looked smaller, but they seemed to fit snugly into their surroundings, providing a completely different picture to the one I was used to at ground level.

Whether in geography or human nature, distance undoubtedly produces a clearer and fuller picture. And it is amazing how hindsight always displays the sharpest visual acuity in the many and varying situations of life. Yet unfortunately, distance or hindsight are rarely available to us when we feel we could do with them most.

Instead, our proximity to a developing situation can stop us from seeing what lies both beside and beyond it: our focus is held resolutely on what is going on in our immediate vicinity. Difficult circumstances can overwhelm us, possessing our waking thoughts and disturbing our sleep, eventually becoming all-consuming. Accompanying feelings of being trapped ensure we only see the walls of heartache that make up our prison, and there seems to be no clear way of escape. Any thought of what that same pain could *positively* produce in us and through us is usually foreign to our thoughts at such a time.

Our perspective, therefore, is altered because we simply cannot see the "big picture", even though we are firmly placed within it.

It is also easy at times like these for relatively minor things to be blown out of all proportion, transforming the proverbial molehill into a mountain, with the resultant damage to our inner peace. Often that is because we have not taken a step back to give ourselves the distance that is required to put things into perspective. Usually a good night's sleep, wise counsel from a friend, sensible reassessment of the situation, all accompanied by prayer, will often reduce the "mountain" back to a more manageable size. The situation, put into perspective once more, can then be dealt with appropriately. Panic over – for now!

Yet there are times when our problems simply are nothing short of "mountains". They loom large above us, casting a shadow of gargantuan proportions across our lives; their dark presence is a devastating daily reality. Much of our coping strategy has been used up, or is totally inappropriate for what we face. Where does perspective fit in, when survival is all we care about?

Does gaining perspective even matter?

The prophet Isaiah discovered that it does, and that it puts a helpful and healing slant on things, for either climbing those "mountains" or seeing them moved (Matthew 17:20). When his own "mountain" loomed large, Isaiah learnt to see with different eyes. He was already aware of the wise words of Solomon in Ecclesiastes chapter 3, that God has put eternity in our hearts. It is the lens of eternity that puts a different perspective on everything, and lets us see a much bigger picture than the constraints of the present allow.

Isaiah was in the Temple when he first got a glimpse of God's big picture for his life. Not unusual, you might say, for a prophet of God. But this time was different for Isaiah. The trouble-free, prosperous life of the nobility that he had enjoyed up until that point was now falling down around him. The king had died. But for Isaiah, King Uzziah was more than his monarch – he was also his cousin and his friend. Isaiah's sense of personal loss was great and his grief was deep.

In the years leading up to King Uzziah's death, the nation had become weakened by immorality. Drunkenness was a national pastime, greedy landlords abused the poor and the Lord Jehovah was rejected by a people no longer able to distinguish between good and evil.

Isaiah was therefore overwhelmed, not only by personal sadness, but also by national sin. And to make matters worse, an international crisis was developing around their borders, which he knew would decimate the southern kingdom of Judah. Threatened by such a "mountain" of disaster, Isaiah found himself in the Temple, in the place where he knew he could find God.

Whilst there, he was given the privilege of seeing through different eyes.

Undoubtedly, he had been in the Temple on many occasions, but on this particular day something was to happen that would not only impact him personally, but would have a profound effect on the nation of Judah – and on mankind forever.

Grief and despair formed the catalyst that sent Isaiah to the Temple with a different attitude of heart: one which would result in an encounter with God that the years of prosperity had never brought. For on that most dreadful of all days ... Isaiah *saw* the Lord, and it changed him forever!

Recorded in chapter 6 of his prophecy, Isaiah describes in graphic detail the sight before him. It was awesome, frightening, challenging and comforting all in one. This man, whose thoughts had been on the death of an earthly king, was transported to see and even be part of the vision and reality of a Heavenly King – all-powerful, unstoppable and eternal.

A glimpse at God's unsurpassed sovereignty involved imagery that took Isaiah's breath away: "I saw the Lord sitting on a throne, high and lifted up, and the train of His robe filled the temple" (Isaiah 6:1). This King was not waited on by mere footmen, but rather by angelic beings, whose voices shook the doorposts as they declared the holiness of God.

At that moment, this remarkable encounter with God produced great fear in Isaiah. The reality of God's holiness matched the power that left Isaiah initially awestruck, and suddenly he was terrified by his own sin and inadequacy in the presence of such holiness: "Woe is me ... Because I am a man of unclean lips ... For my eyes have seen the King, the LORD of hosts" (Isaiah 6:5).

In his declaration of who God is, combined with the recognition of his own sinful nature, Isaiah then experienced the mercy and cleansing of God, enabling him to continue in God's presence – for God had more to say!

Yet when the time came for Isaiah to leave that special place, his grief was still there; the nation was still under threat; the people were still God-rejecters and consumed by their sinful practices. So what had changed? What was the purpose in this close encounter with God if everything was still the same?

Isaiah was the one who had changed!

He now had a completely different perspective on all that was going on around him. God was not only more real to him; he was sure of his position in God's big plan, and more importantly, he knew that the mountain *would* eventually be moved. For the present, the darkness would deepen, and the nation would crumble under the weight of God's judgment, but in future days Isaiah was to become God's messenger of the good news of deliverance for the people of Judah. The good news Isaiah was to declare also contained the best news ever for all of mankind, for in Isaiah 53 we read of Jesus, our suffering Saviour, the One who was "wounded for our transgressions ... bruised for our iniquities" (verse 5).

Is it any wonder that Isaiah was never the same again?

God had a plan! That plan included deliverance, mercy and hope – and that plan included Isaiah. With his new vision of God firmly embedded in his heart, Isaiah saw that the plan was about more than merely the present. It had eternal consequences that enabled him to see through different eyes.

Often there have been times when I have asked God to let me ride on His shoulders, convinced that if I could only catch a glimpse of His big picture for my life, the pain would be easier to bear. That's not possible at the minute. Instead I have discovered that, just like Isaiah, my hard times make me run to Him, and with each encounter I have had, I have seen Him with a fresh vision. The here and now has been touched by the eternal. Amazingly, that's when I see through different eyes.

The year following Cheryl's diagnosis could be likened to competing on an assault course. We seemed to survive one obstacle only to have the next looming directly in front of us. Hospital appointments came in batches! The number of health professionals who wanted to visit our tiny home seemed ridiculous at times. And while we were grateful for all the help we could get, none of them seemed to bring any encouraging news. Our particular assault course always seemed to involve blood, sweat and tears.

"Your daughter has cortical blindness," was one obstacle I hadn't seen coming.

On an afternoon I will never forget, my husband dropped us off at the front entrance of the hospital on his way to speak at a meeting. Trying to reassure him that I would be fine on my own with Cheryl, I quipped: "I'm not expecting anything mind-blowing today – don't worry. See you later."

By the time we reached the busy eye clinic, Cheryl was fast asleep. And she was totally unimpressed when a brusque nurse pulled down her lower eyelids to insert stinging drops!

"She needs to have her pupils dilated before the doctor sees her," was the nurse's curt explanation as she pointed to a dimly lit room where we were supposed to take a seat.

The room was crowded on three sides, the previous silence now broken by the screams of one very unhappy baby. Squashing in between two adults, I tried to calm Cheryl whilst taking in my surroundings. I noticed that from time to time patients would enter the two curtained cubicles occupying the unseated area of the square room, and I was shocked that all present could hear every word of what should have been a private consultation.

With Cheryl in one arm and pushing the buggy with the other, I entered the small "cloth box" when her name was called. Following the briefest of looks at the referral letter, the young doctor rushed off through an adjoining door, leaving the curtain undrawn. After some time had passed, the door opened and a man, whom I assumed was the consultant, appeared with a large entourage of medical students, and the aforesaid doctor.

"There's no way they are all going to fit into such a small space," I thought.

They didn't! They just left the curtains undrawn and our lives open and vulnerable to the unwilling audience seated around us.

"So you are concerned about her sight?" the doctor asked. Then without waiting for a reply, he turned to the waiting students: "What do you notice about this child?" he grunted, adding an impatient, "Come on – it's very obvious!"

"Her head is small – flat at the back," someone replied.

"Exactly!" smiled the specialist, without the slightest hesitation about what he was going to say about the smallest patient he would see that day.

I felt invisible! My daughter was being used as a teaching tool, more akin to a plastic model than a living child. The atmosphere in the room was embarrassingly tense, the other people longing for a big hole to swallow them up as the doctor insensitively continued to give his public lecture on what was wrong with *my* child.

Finally he turned to me for the first time and said, "Your daughter has cortical blindness; nothing wrong with her eyes, her brain just can't make sense of what is coming through them. No need to make another appointment – there isn't anything we can do for her."

Then with a flick of the hand, a path was cleared for his exit!

And I was left to pick up the pieces. Another devastating diagnosis – another chip knocked off my already battered heart.

The journey to the car was memorable. Pouring rain helped to disguise my tears as I negotiated Cheryl's pushchair through the busy streets to meet up with my husband.

Thankfully, the journey to God's heart was much easier to navigate. From the back seat of our car, I once again poured out my woes, laced with anger and unfairness. I was met with silence. It wasn't an uncomfortable, condemning silence, but rather, a quiet understanding that brought great comfort; a wrap-around sense of a Father's love, a physical outworking of Deuteronomy 33:27: "The eternal God is your refuge, And underneath are the everlasting arms". An overwhelmingly tangible sense of God's peace ran over me, like a bucket of cool water on a hot day, relieving my every sense.

As I eventually stopped struggling and rested in those everlasting arms, I began to see through different eyes, recognizing, in those moments, God as my Father. His tender heart was indeed my refuge; my place of safety. There would always be foolish people to add to my hurt, but my vision of Him was growing larger every day, helping me put things into perspective.

For whatever, and whoever, the future held, I knew then that I could run to Him at any time, because the truth had begun to dawn: whatever was going on, God had a plan – and I was part of it.

Comparisons – avoiding the pitfalls

Our children are constantly comparing themselves to their peers. From early days they notice what others have and, if it appears better than what they have, somehow they feel that they are losing out.

Whilst the desire not to be different is strong amongst the young, the ramifications of measuring your life and possessions against those of others can have hurtful consequences. Children have been bullied for something as trivial as not wearing the "accepted" brand of trainers.

This behaviour is not confined to the young, nor can it be explained as simply part of growing up. The trend of not wanting to stand out as different continues into adulthood. Consequently, making comparisons has become a national pastime.

The size of our house; the area we live in; our employment or lack of it; the make and model of car we drive; the type of holiday we take; the school our children attend, all have the potential of influencing how we see others, and they us. Even subconsciously we are lured into making comparisons, such is the powerful hold achievement and acceptance exert on us. And from that, judgments can be made, or should I say assumptions, as to our worth as human beings.

If our self-worth has taken a blow, or is something we regularly struggle with, we can easily fall into the trap of believing the message fed to us from various directions.

"Bigger is best!" we are told.

"You're worth it!" the advertisements shout at us as they encourage us to buy their brands.

"Why should your children not have the best in electronic gadgetry?" the credit companies say, while offering to extend our credit limit.

These subliminal messages of materialism then cause us to justify the comparisons we make, often leading to discontent or feelings of failure. After all, the more you have of "things", money, intelligence, or good looks, the more likely you are to be accepted by society than someone who has less. Therefore, if my house is smaller than yours, then I obviously have some way to go on the social ladder that seems to be permanently perched against my life.

Unfortunately this pitfall of comparison can end in pain. Relationships have been damaged because of discontent; marriages have been ruined because of money worries caused by credit card debt; businesses have failed at the cost of personal health; and children have become self-centred, learning from the behaviour of parents who are desperately trying to "keep up with the Joneses".

Yet which of us has not looked up from the depths of this dreadful pit at some time or other?

As we had started off our married life in Christian service, I had never known anything other than living on a low income. And that was fine. I worked part-time hours after the children came along, and that helped with our household circumstances. We were very content – until I took a well-paid job some years later when our son was heading off to music college in London. The job was certainly

God's provision for what was a difficult financial time in our lives, and it allowed Paul to complete his studies debt free.

As the time of his graduation approached, I was shocked at how often my thoughts were turning to how we could use the money that had previously gone to Paul every month. I became excited at the thought of buying things we had never been previously able to afford. In my quieter moments I would daydream about being able to save for our retirement, my husband's pension provision being paltry. Yet alongside all this excitement about money, I was ashamed by my own hedonistic thoughts. God had always provided for our needs in fulfilment of Philippians 4:19 and our standard of living had never troubled me – until now.

It felt like the end of an era when Paul returned home for the last time as a student, before entering his final term. Normally, once his case landed on the bedroom floor, he'd collapse into an armchair, ready to begin the big "catch-up" of all the happenings while he'd been away. But on this occasion he dropped a book into my lap before heading for a seat. Nothing too unusual really, as Paul and I always enjoyed checking out each other's reading when he was at home. What was unusual, though, was the excitement with which he spoke about the book I was now fingering.

"You've got to read this, Mum!" he said. "It's mind-blowing! Probably the most challenging book I've read, next to the Bible." He continued to wax eloquent about the book, which was entitled *Your God is Too Safe* by Mark Buchanan.[1] Scanning through the contents list with Paul's voice in the background, I determined that this was one book I needed to read, even if only to discover why it had engaged my son so dramatically.

But before too long I was wishing that Paul hadn't given me that book!

Or at least that's how I felt during the times when its words were doing their work on my soul. Paul was right – it was unputdownable! And uncomfortable reading for the most part, especially with what was going on in my life at that time. Through its pages my knowledge of God was enlarged and many of my life-choices were challenged by the author. Was my day-to-day living focused on me, or was it surrendered to God? Did I want my relationship with God to be safe – but boring – or was I prepared to step out of my comfort zone to live the kind of exciting life God had intended me to live?

Soon my personal desires were playing tug-of-war with God's plan for my life.

Ultimately it was God's voice, through the words of Romans 12:2, that spoke even louder than those of Mark Buchanan. In the cool light of day I may have been able to rationalize the words of another mortal, but not so with God's Word. It is totally inerrant!

"Don't copy the behaviour and customs of this world, *Catherine*, but let God transform you into a new person by changing the way you think. Then you will learn to know God's will for you, which is good and pleasing and perfect" (NLT, italics mine).

The message to my heart was as clear as the ink on the page. What this world offers cannot be compared with the good, pleasing and perfect will of God. There is simply no contest! And so, with my hands firmly placed on the rungs of the social ladder that was tempting me to climb higher, I pushed it away from my life, asking God to transform me by changing the way that I thought.

A few months later I resigned from my job, happily and willingly, in response to God's call to extend my ministry of speaking and writing.

I wish I could say that the pitfalls of comparisons are limited to the measurable in our lives. But, unfortunately, they go beyond bricks, cars and bank accounts, to the things of the heart.

In fact, there appears to be a cruel hierarchy of pain. Somewhere, in our psyche, lurks an unwritten list that categorizes suffering. It is in common usage. I've heard the words myself on numerous occasions: "Oh, that's awful, but it's not as bad as so-and-so – did you hear what happened to them?" "Not as bad as ..." Yet can we really say that the infidelity of a partner is less painful than if they had died? Or that the death of a father is to be preferred over the death of a mother – if the children are still small? Who knows whether the loss of one's business is easier to accept than the loss of one's health? Is it really right to say that death from chronic illness is a relief, but a sudden death is a disaster?

And at the top of the pile, we are told that there is *nothing* that can compare with the death of a child. It has been made the plumb line against which all other pain is measured.

This has caused me great concern. By this time I was heavily involved in my speaking ministry; both of our daughters had died. Since I am often asked to speak on some aspect of suffering, my own personal circumstances are well known to those gathered. This often leads to difficulty when people try to share their own personal heartache with me.

I have been disturbed to see an elderly lady, whose husband is ravaged with dementia, angry at her own distress, because she regards her experience "as nothing compared to what you have come through!". My heart was broken as I listened to a young woman apologize for crying, because her husband's infidelity "cannot be compared with the death of your child!".

Yet, God has no such list of comparisons. Rather, He treats us all the same. For when our Heavenly Father declares Himself as "close to the broken-hearted, and [a rescuer of] those who are crushed in spirit" (Psalm 34:18 NIV), the cause of the pain is not mentioned. His concern is only with our broken heart, and how it can be healed.

Making comparisons is not the same as putting things into perspective. It should be as foreign to our thinking as it is to the Bible's teaching. Instead we need to have our attitudes transformed – and only God can do that, by changing the way we think.

How big is God?

Children ask the most amazing questions, don't they?

There are the investigative questions, such as: "How did the baby get inside your tummy, Mummy?" or "How does Santa get down the chimney?" The sad questions: "Why does my friend not like me any more?" or "Can Grandad come back from Heaven to visit us?" Then there are the searching questions: "Why can't I see God?" or "Why did God not make my daddy better?" or "How big is God, Mummy?"

At certain stages in their development the questioning of our children never seems to end! And it requires the wisdom of Solomon to decide what is actually being asked and how much information is really required from the answer. Undoubtedly, questions are a healthy sign of growth. Once correctly answered, they can expand the knowledge and confidence required to reach maturity, and are not merely to satisfy curiosity.

It works just the same in our Christian lives. As children of God, we grow towards maturity by asking questions. Our desire for more knowledge concerning all facets of living in God's family should be insatiable. Yet to mature, we require more than the knowledge of facts. We require the wisdom to apply them to our everyday lives – especially when our fault line shakes and disaster strikes. It is at these times when the big questions are most often asked. And the answers to those big questions are vital when we are trying to gain perspective at a time of confusion and pain.

Next to the "Why me?" question comes the "How big is God?" question. In reality, perhaps the question needs to be rephrased: "How big is God in my estimation?" The answer to such a question does not require theological training, or in-depth Bible knowledge, or even a quick telephone call to the pastor! Instead, the answer is seen in how we live our everyday lives. Do we pray *big* prayers, believing that God is able to answer them? Or do we stay well within the safety zone, praying for the probable whilst avoiding the humanly impossible? Does our walk of faith require a safety net – preferably of our own making – just in case God doesn't come through for us? Have we put God on some sort of trial? Do we imagine that if this "Christianity thing" doesn't work out, then it can be as easily dropped as a new brand of soap?

Often our need to be in control, or at the very least, to understand how everything works around us, identifies us as people who have a very small estimation of God. Our desire to live safely, rather than by faith, not only results in spiritual boredom, it inadequately prepares us for the time when all our little man-made props are taken away. Then suddenly, the God we say we trust in doesn't seem big enough for our problems.

That's certainly how ten of the spies sent out by Moses to reconnoitre the Promised Land felt. In their estimation God just wasn't big enough for all that they expected to face if called on to advance into Canaan. That disbelief caused mutiny, death and forty more years of wandering in the wilderness.

Not all of the spies, however, brought back the same report. They had started out as a band of twelve brave men – not ten. They were all young leaders from eleven of the twelve tribes of Israel, and including one whose trust in God was only matched by that of Joshua, the man who would eventually replace Moses. His name was Caleb.

Caleb could feel his heart beating loudly in his chest as he stood in line. The tribe of Judah looked on with pride as they witnessed their strong, fearless leader stand before Moses and Aaron. Yet Caleb's strength did not only lie in his warrior physique, but in his unshakable faith in the Lord Jehovah who had delivered them a few years earlier from the slavery of the cruel Egyptians.

The vast crowd before him seemed to sway like the waves of the sea as they waited for Moses to speak. Caleb smiled as he watched "the waves" part, as his own children jostled and manoeuvred to get into a good position from which to view the line-up of Israel's finest. He was glad to see excitement rather than fear in their young faces: evidence that they had been listening to him after all. He had been straight with them – this would be a dangerous mission. But at the recent Passover feast he had made a point of telling them that the God who had rescued them from Egypt had promised Canaan for their inheritance. So they did not need to be afraid of the job their father had been chosen to do.

The warm breeze whipped up the sand around them. Wiping his face, Caleb looked forward to the day when sand would not feature in his life. And if what he had heard of Canaan was true, then he could also look forward to grapes and pomegranates as an accompaniment to his food instead of this bothersome dust! He could almost taste the juicy fruit in his mouth as Moses held out his staff to quiet the people.

Straightening in response, Caleb was aware of the men standing alongside him, who would accompany him on this scouting venture. To his right stood Igal, from Joseph's descent; to his left stood Shammua, the son of Zaccur. Then beside him was Hoshea of Ephraim's tribe – the mission could not fail with his great friend on board! But Caleb corrected himself as he remembered that Moses had given Hoshea a new name. From now on he would be called Joshua, which meant "The Lord is salvation". It suited him, Caleb thought. Moses was wise indeed, for every time one of the men called out Joshua's name they would be reminded that the Lord would save them out of any and every situation.

Moses' voice interrupted Caleb's thoughts, drawing his attention once more: "Go north", God's chosen leader of Israel began, "through the Negev into the hill country" (Numbers 13:17 NLT).

Short, straightforward instructions followed from Israel's great leader. "See what the land is like, and find out whether the people living there are strong or weak, few or many. See what kind of land they live in. Is it good or bad? Do their towns have walls, or are they unprotected like open camps? Is the soil fertile or poor? Are there many trees?" (verses 18–20 NLT).

Caleb could see some of the other men nod in agreement as Moses continued with a request that drew a smile across Caleb's face.

"Enter the land boldly, and bring back samples of the crops you see" (verse 20 NLT).

Crossing his arms with pride at the humble leader's request, Caleb recognized what Moses was up to. Tempting this host of moaners and groaners with samples of "real" food would undoubtedly entice them to move ahead into the land that had been described years earlier by God Himself as "flowing with milk and honey" (Exodus 3:8 NLT). Moses may not have been a military man, but his wisdom in the moving of a nation was something Caleb greatly admired.

Now, with Moses' blessing ringing in his ears, and the shouts of the tribes of Israel causing the ground to shake beneath their feet, the spies headed off towards the north.

Caleb draped his rough woollen cloak over his left shoulder, a goatskin of fresh water settling into the small of his back and a little sack of food attached to the belt holding his linen kilt in place. Their Egyptian clothing would hopefully make them look more like passing traders than spies from a huge nation waiting to invade the land they were now about to reconnoitre.

With the wilderness of Paran behind, Caleb and his comrades passed the lush, waving palm trees of Kadesh Barnea. The beautiful oasis was providing life-giving water for over a million of his people at that time. How he thanked God for such an amazing provision. Completely unconcerned by the task ahead, the men's spirits were high … full of excitement and expectancy, fuelled by bravado. And as those first miles of barren, rocky paths were crossed, the spies spoke together of what it would be like to walk on grassy slopes. The harsh wilderness of rock and sand was their bridge to the lush land of Canaan. In their estimation, each difficult step taken was more than worth the effort.

As they walked, Caleb and Joshua talked together of the privilege that was soon to be theirs. The prospect of being the first to view the land promised to their forefathers by the Lord Jehovah filled them with excitement, pumping adrenaline through their bodies. The early miles passed quickly, and soon Beersheba was in sight.

Arriving at Canaan's southernmost border town, the men blended in easily with their surroundings. Beersheba was more of a watering-hole than a town, where those travelling the trade route to Egypt, along with local shepherds, used the well to quench their thirst and refresh their animals. And this is exactly what the twelve spies did, refilling their water bottles for the long journey that still had to be covered. Resting by the well, Caleb couldn't help but think of the patriarch Abraham as he had set off from that very place one fateful day to offer up his son Isaac as a sacrifice to God. As the story he had heard as a boy played on Caleb's mind, a smile crossed his face. He remembered that eventually God Himself provided a sacrifice – Isaac was spared because God made a way out for Abraham.

"God made a way out for us too," Caleb muttered, pictures of the Red Sea parting now rising in his mind's eye. "What are you muttering about, Caleb?" Igal said, throwing a piece of bread at his friend to bring him back from his daydreaming.

Playfully throwing the bread back in Igal's direction, Caleb stood to his feet, gathering up his belongings as he replied.

"I was thinking about our mighty God, Igal … and looking forward to getting on with this journey!"

Taking the hint, the men rose to their feet and headed on once more. The next stages of the journey could prove to be more dangerous. Word of what had happened in Egypt a few years earlier would undoubtedly have reached Canaan from travellers in the region. And it is hard to hide more than a million people, even in the inhospitable wilderness of Zin. The spies realized that the peoples of Canaan were already aware of a nation camping on their borders, and would be expecting trouble sooner or later.

The climb to Hebron stretched their endurance a little, sitting as it does at the highest point of the surrounding countryside. But the twelve were used to covering difficult terrain, having spent time around Mount Sinai after leaving Egypt. As they climbed towards the town, Caleb and the others were able to view this land given to Abraham and his offspring in a covenant promise by God so many years before.

Also I give to you and your descendants after you the land in which you are a stranger, all the land of Canaan, as an everlasting possession; and I will be their God.

GENESIS 17:8

The view was breathtaking, the promise powerful!

For the majority of the group, however, the excitement was quickly replaced by fear, and confidence in the promise of God disappeared in the mountain mist.

"Look at the size of these men!" shouted one of the spies as they watched people come and go through the town gate.

"They must be descendants of Anak!" another continued. "We are like grasshoppers beside them!"

Panic now started to fill the hearts of the group that had begun so well. Returning quickly to their hillside hideout, the men started to complain about the impossibility of defeating a population of such tall, strong men. Caleb and Joshua sat in disbelief around the campfire as they heard words such as "Nephilim" (giants) come from the mouths of their companions. They could not dispute that the Anakim would be a fierce foe, but attributing their descent to the Nephilim was a step too far. Caleb and Joshua tried to reason with the others and calm the situation, explaining that the evil giant race known as the Nephilim was destroyed in the flood of Noah's day. Anyway, what were the inhabitants of Hebron compared to God; it was they who were grasshoppers beside Him! Had He not rolled back the Red Sea, delivered them from the Egyptians, and provided food and water for over a million people in the wilderness? "We must finish the job we were given to do," Joshua pleaded. "Our children are depending on us. God will give us victory and take care of us."

Wrapping his cloak around him against the chilly mountain air, Caleb rolled up beside a nearby rock, moaning in disbelief. He had thought that this group of men – of all people – would not doubt that God would keep His promise and give them this land. At least they had agreed to continue with their mission.

Managing to walk around ten to twelve miles a day, the spies continued northwards. Having left Hebron behind, Caleb could sense that their group was splitting into two, with a rather unbalanced divide: ten to two. Apart from Joshua and himself, the other ten were becoming more negative with every passing day. Even the grapes, pomegranates and figs they were able to gather and enjoy in the Valley of Eschol did nothing to encourage the doubters amongst them.

Weary after their long journey from Hebron to Shechem, the complaining grew worse. Most of the towns they had passed were fortified to some degree or another. It appears that the "ten" had thought God would just expect them to walk into Canaan and claim it without any serious opposition, so as mile followed mile they were simply confirmed in their conviction that the task would be too hard for them – and for God!

By the time they left the fortified city of Beth-shean behind and arrived at Hazor, the ten were totally overwhelmed by the sight in front of them. Hazor was bigger and better fortified than any city they had seen up until that point. It looked more like two cities rather than one. The spies could see that they would first have to capture the lower city of 160 acres, before storming the stone-and-mudbrick walls, twenty-four feet wide, to reach the upper city, which covered an extra twenty-six acres. In the minds of the ten it was totally impossible – but not so with Caleb and Joshua.

These two faithful men kept on trying to reassure the other ten that they would not be expected to conquer Canaan alone. God had promised to be with them … therefore they could not fail! Yes, the problems in Canaan were huge – but God was bigger. Neither the descendants of Anak, nor the walls of Hazor posed too great a threat with the Lord Jehovah on their side! But the encouraging words of Caleb and Joshua fell on deaf ears. Even the sight of fertile agricultural land did not entice the ten men, and the taste of ripe fruit turned sour in their stomachs in light of what they had discovered along the way.

After reaching Rehob in the far north of Canaan, the twelve spies turned and set off for home: ten dejected, two elated. And the report they would give on their return would have devastating consequences for over a million homeless people.

The majority report told of giants in the land, of people "stronger than we are", of "cities ... fortified and very large"... and concluded "we felt like grasshoppers next to them" (Numbers 13:31, 28, 33 NLT). A few words stating that the land "truly flows with milk and honey" (verse 27) were the only positive comment from the ten men, who said nothing about God anywhere in their report.

Caleb was horrified!

Barely able to contain himself, he interrupted the ten with the words: "Let us go at once to take the land ... We can certainly conquer it!" (verse 30 NLT).

But his words were to no avail. The ten had sown fear and unbelief amongst the Children of Israel with their words of discouragement. They believed they would never be able to take the land – and God didn't even come into the picture. In their eyes He simply wasn't big enough for the job!

The sound of weeping filled the desert all night. The people plotted against Moses and Aaron ... *and even suggested going back to Egypt*! They refused to believe that God would give them the land ... refused to believe that the God who had not only rescued them from Egypt but stopped the enemy from pursuing them, would be able to deliver on His promise.

Having travelled almost 500 miles in a period lasting forty days, Caleb and Joshua were desperate to encourage the people to trust in God. They made one brave final attempt to convince them, giving their all as they spoke passionately to the community of Israel:

"The land we explored is a wonderful land! And if the LORD is pleased with us, He will bring us safely into that land and give it to us. It is a rich land flowing with milk and honey, and He will give it to us! Do not rebel against the LORD, and don't be afraid of the people of the land. They are only helpless prey to us! They have no protection, but the LORD is with us! Don't be afraid of them!" (Numbers 14:7–9 NLT).

Caleb stood in silence, waiting for the crowd's reply, convinced that their words would turn the hearts of the people. And turn them they certainly did – against him and his friend Joshua! It wasn't long before they realized that the people wanted them silenced for good. Yet before a stone could be thrown against them, God's glorious presence appeared from above the Tent of Meeting, protecting His two faithful servants.

It would be another forty years before Joshua and Caleb would again set foot in Canaan. Unbelief, rebellion and pride would keep the Children of Israel out of the Promised Land. Those who saw God as too small to deal with the "giants" in the land never had the privilege of setting foot on the lush Valley of Eshcol, or of watching the sun set from the hillside of Hebron.

But Caleb had what God called "a different spirit in him" (Numbers 14:24). He was able to trust God fully because he looked at the situation from a different perspective. Yes, he saw the giants. Yes, he saw the fortified cities. Yes, he knew it wouldn't be easy – but he also saw God! And the God Caleb saw towered above the giants and made *them* look like grasshoppers! He was unafraid of anything that the Canaanites might throw at them, because he was absolutely convinced that there was nothing else to compare with God's might.

How was it that Caleb and Joshua saw things differently from the others? Surely all twelve of the spies had come out of Egypt; all twelve of them had tasted the manna and eaten the quail as it fell from the sky? Each one had witnessed the water gushing from the rock, and had seen Moses' face shine when he came down the mountain after meeting with God. What made the difference?

Why did only two of them believe that God could take them safely into Canaan?

It was because Caleb and Joshua had gained a different perspective.

They had chosen to remember all that God had done for them in the past, which in turn helped them to trust Him with the promises He had given them for the future. It was that simple – they believed God. And they believed that He was bigger, and more powerful, than anything they faced in the present or anything they might ever encounter in the future.

Their God was a big God!

I don't know about you, but there are times when my "forgettery" works much better than my memory! And it is at those times that I can become anxious. Doubt worries its way into my heart, and if I'm not careful, my perspective of God's ability can shift – resulting in an unbelief that makes Him small in my eyes. The result of such action can be catastrophic, depriving me of peace and forcing me to meet "giants" that I should never have to deal with alone.

Sometimes physical tiredness or emotional exhaustion act like keys, locking up the memories that are so helpful in expanding trust and changing perspective. To help combat this problem, I write things down and let the ink do the remembering for me. It could be a Bible verse that God used to minister to me at a particularly difficult time, or a card sent by a friend, or the words of a hymn, or a special date, or a photograph, or a pressed flower. Then, when my "forgettery" starts causing me to doubt whether or not God can handle that "giant" of grief, or that "fortification" of disappointment, I reach for my little red book and remind myself of all that God has done for me in the past. Before long, those memories help me to put things into proper perspective once more, and I discover that God is undoubtedly big and powerful!

Caleb and Joshua actually experienced the miracles of the Exodus, and gained knowledge from the stories told to them by their fathers, but we now have the vastness of God's Word to draw from. Add to this the assurance that the power that raised Jesus from the dead is available to us, and surely we can never doubt God's ability – whatever we might face!

Therefore, if, in the future, my little granddaughter asks, "How big is God, Granny?", I can safely reply: "Bigger than anything you might ever see or could ever imagine, sweetheart!"

God in pain

I visited the cross today.

And I wept at the sight I saw!

It was a magazine article I was writing that transported me to stand in the darkness, outside Jerusalem, at that Passover Feast so many years ago. I looked through the eyes of my character at the Son of God hanging on a Roman gibbet, and the old shepherd I was writing about wasn't the only one sobbing.

Jesus' face was bloated and bruised beyond recognition. Dried blood crusted around the holes made by the mocking crown of long Eastern thorns that pushed into His brow. The sinews of His flesh strained against the pull of the nails that pinned His body to the wood, while His ribs desperately tried to expand the lungs of the incarnate Saviour of the world. The very air could not find a way in to rescue the One who had created it. The purple bruises inflicted by His cruel executioners were the only covering left on Jesus' naked body – shame added to the agony He had to endure.

The old shepherd and I watched – as the crowds jeered, the women cried, the earth shook, and darkness blackened the sky at noon.

We saw God in pain!

The shepherd was surprised at first … to see the One whom the angel had told him about, hanging on a cross. But not me: I knew why Jesus was there. I could hear the words of John the Baptist reaching down through the centuries to my heart: "Behold! The Lamb of God who takes away the sin of the world!" (John 1:29).

I didn't want to look – it was all too terrible! But my eyes were fixed on Him.

And the one thing I couldn't get away from was what Jesus was saying ... with His last earthly breaths:

"Father, forgive them, for they do not know what they do" (Luke 23:34).

And I was overwhelmed by His love!

When our son was small we used to play a little game. "How much do you love me, Mummy?" he would say impishly. Holding his chubby little hands a few inches apart, he would try to put a measurement on my love. "Do you love me this much?"

"Oh, no," I would reply, "much more than that!" "How about this, Mummy? Do you love me this much?"

As the game continued he would hold his hands wider and wider apart and each time I would reply: "Oh, no, I love you much more than that!"

Eventually he would stand in front of me on tiptoes, with arms stretched taut and fingers reaching for the walls, his very face grimacing with the effort.

"Do you love me this much, then, Mummy?"

"Oh, no!" I would reply, the pair of us hardly able to contain our giggles. "I love you this much!" – my own, much longer arms stretching far beyond what he could manage.

Then he would run into my outstretched arms with delight, assured of the enormity of my love for him.

One day, when he had been naughty, and had received a telling off for his misdemeanour, he slunk away remorsefully. I left him to his thoughts. In a short time he returned with tears welling up in his eyes.

"Do you even love me this much, Mummy?" he said hopefully, holding his small hands inches apart.

"No!" I replied firmly.

The word threw him, causing his chin to tremble.

"I love you this much, Paul!" I said, stretching my arms wider than I had ever managed before. "Whatever you do cannot change how much your mummy loves you!"

In seconds my errant son was wrapped in my arms. On that day, as I held him close, I could hear Another whisper in my ear: *"That's how much I love you too, Catherine!"*

There are times when we might doubt the depth of God's love for us. Pain, sorrow, rejection, even sin, may dim our perception somewhat. Those looking on can also be confused as to how we are dealing with our pain. On a number of occasions I have been asked the question: "Catherine, how can you trust in a God who has allowed so much heartache in your life?"

I find that an easy question to answer, especially on a day when I have taken time to visit the cross.

"Jesus is no stranger to pain," I explain. "He knows exactly how I feel. And when I wonder how much He loves me, one look at His outstretched arms tells me all that I need to know!"

Trust follows easily on the heels of love.

The magazine article is finished: the "send" button has been pressed. The cross has been visited once more.

Yet as my fingers tap on the keyboard, I know that I should come here more often, because the cross is the one place that puts everything else into perspective.

Notes
1. Mark Buchanan, *Your God is Too Safe*, Multnomah Publishers, 2001.

Taking a closer look

- Read Ecclesiastes 3:11b. How does this verse help us to gain perspective in our everyday lives?

- Consider a time when you saw God differently than you ever had before. Does that experience still impact your life? If not, why not? Perhaps reading Isaiah 6:1–8 will help.

- Read Romans 12:2 in a couple of different Bible versions. Respond honestly to what God is saying to you through these words.

- If someone were to listen in to your prayers, how big would they reckon your God to be? Would Matthew 21:21–22 be evident?

- Read Caleb's story for yourself in the Old Testament books of Numbers (chapters 13 and 14) and Deuteronomy (chapter 1).

- Visit the cross today from any or all of these references: Matthew 27:32–54; Mark 15:22–39; Luke 23:26–46; John 19:16–37.

THREE

DOES GOD CARE?

How does God see me?

"Does God see me at all?"

"Does He even know I exist?"

"In fact, does *anyone* know I exist?"

"I'm nobody special; why would God bother about me?"

These are all real questions that I have been asked at one time or another. Questions that show how little value individuals seem to place on their own lives; questions that show how little they believe God cares about them.

Recently, a young man interviewed for a news report concerning British unemployment figures passionately stated to camera: "I don't want to be a statistic! I want to *be* somebody – to make something of my life!"

My heart went out to him. I was sympathetic to his jobless plight, and understood what he was trying to say. However, I was more saddened by the message behind his statement. His identity was all tied up with *doing* and not with who he was. In his opinion, to be "somebody" meant having a job. He didn't have a job; therefore he was a "nobody" – a mere statistic. "Making something of his life" was all to do with how others would see him. He wanted to be noticed; to be valued by society. The young man was describing that inbuilt desire we all have to feel significant in the lives of others. Even those of a quieter disposition require the approval of others to boost their self-esteem.

Consequently, achievement and recognition have become the means by which we measure whether we matter to someone: a method of reaching out to discover if anyone really cares about us. Unfortunately, using this approach may force us to conclude that attention from others is a reward, to be granted only if "I make something of myself".

The "age of celebrity" in which we live further discourages those who struggle with feelings of worthlessness or invisibility. Finding our true identity eludes us more often than not because of the trend to place exceptional acclaim on those whom society promotes as the real achievers of our day. By the use of technology, the rich and famous can even become our "friends" through social media networks. We can follow their every move and be shown what they want us to see of the kind of life we would wish to aspire to.

Individuals become brands, being transformed into mere marketing opportunities to entice us into their world. However, the term "friends" can only ever be in parenthesis. We do not really know these famous people – we only know the brand their agent is presenting. The personality of the real individual could be far distant from what we have imagined them to be.

Running alongside celebrity-watching is the phenomenon of reality television, whose programmes attract huge audiences. Thousands of people will queue for hours to take part in an audition which may only last for a few minutes, or even seconds. Many of the "wannabes" will go through humiliation, prepared to be laughed at by millions in the hope of reaching their goal – that of becoming famous. They will risk the pain of rejection and crushed dreams for the chance that someone, somewhere, will remember their name.

"What's in a name?" you may ask. An awful lot, it seems!

Knowing a person's name, after all, is the first step towards building relationship. Relationships strengthen our self-esteem and accord a degree of value to our lives. A Christian worker once told a teacher-training class that a child without a name is like a child without a face! We can be left feeling invisible if our personal identity tag is left unused, or worse still, unknown.

There are few of us who don't know how that feels.

It was a normal Saturday shift in the Belfast hospital in which I was working. A ward full of patients and not enough staff was par for the course, and to make matters worse, Sister was on duty! That meant we were down a pair of hands, as Sister rarely left her office.

Almost eight weeks had passed since I had started my placement in the neurology ward, and although only a second-year student nurse, I was finding the specialist unit an interesting and challenging place to work. I thrived on how it was stretching my nursing skills. Every day was extremely busy, working with patients suffering from a variety of disorders and diseases of the brain, some of which I had not even heard of before coming to the ward. So my evenings were also full, looking through the textbooks in search of information relevant to my job. I didn't mind. I simply threw myself into my work, and enjoyed every minute of it. My goal for that period of my life was to be the best nurse that I could possibly be. If that meant working harder than others, then that was what I was prepared to do.

This particular Saturday was no different than any other day. By mid morning we had all run ourselves ragged. Many of the patients were disabled in some way and so required a lot of hands-on nursing care. It was heavy physical work, but a sense of satisfaction descended as the last patient was helped out of bed and comfortably ensconced in an armchair.

Only one more bed to make, and then we could have a tea-break!

Job done, I was wheeling the linen trolley back to its home in the laundry cupboard, and as I passed Sister's office I heard her mention my name. The office door was slightly ajar so I slowed my walk in case she was about to call for me. In fact, the reverse was the case.

"Nurse Fraser?" she repeated loudly down the phone. "I told you before that we do not have anyone of that name working in this ward. Now, don't call again!"

I wanted to push the door open and shout: "I'm Nurse Fraser! I *do* work here! I've *been* working here – very hard – for almost eight weeks!" But I was still a sensitive teenager, and the shock at hearing my current boss tell someone that I didn't exist, sent me running – straight into the linen cupboard! Blocking the door firmly with the heavy stool I had collapsed onto, I summarily burst into tears.

My tired body and aching muscles reassured me that I was not invisible. I was in fact a real person, who had slogged day after day in a busy ward, and who was now realizing that all my hard work would not be rewarded with a good report from the ward Sister. After all, she didn't even know that I existed!

I allowed myself to be overwhelmed by a sense of failure. I had obviously failed to impress the one person who mattered in the ward as far as my training was concerned. All my previous good ward reports would now be damaged by this woman, who had the power to destroy my good name! Exaggerated thinking made a difficult situation worse and I allowed my own personal pity party to continue unabated.

By now my face was puffy and my nose red with crying. I wanted to escape and run for home, but knew that it was hours before that would be possible. Twisting my damp handkerchief ever tighter, I sat in the quietness trying to compose myself before returning to the duties of the day.

"You have found grace in My sight, Catherine, and I know you by name."

I jumped as the words from God's heart broke through the silence and washed over me. I allowed them to sink into my mind, lifting my spirits and bringing my true identity into focus.

"God knows my name!" I repeated a few times. The words of the Lord to Moses in Exodus 33:17b were smothered by the sheets and blankets, but were firmly reinforced in my heart.

"God knows my name, and that's all that matters!"

I began to laugh, realizing that my ward report might be untrue and unfair, but it was of little significance when I acknowledged that my name is known in Heaven. God's report of my life brought identity beyond what I could gain by "doing". He simply cared for me – Catherine, the person – no strings attached.

I am not invisible to Him – He knows my name!

Someone else clearly knew my name, as I heard it from outside the linen-room door: "Catherine, are you all right? We're going for coffee – are you coming?"

"Oh, yes," I replied. "I'm coming!"

To be known for who we are rather than for what we do is liberating.

Millions of people throughout the world cannot study, work, own property or achieve fame, yet each one is of great eternal worth in God's eyes – including you and me. To make this clear, God reminds us in Jeremiah 31:3 that He has loved us with an everlasting love. A love that started before the world was formed, still continues today, and reaches forward into the future. And the verse says nothing about what we have to do to earn it. Exam results, job success or how many other people know our name are totally irrelevant.

And the fact that God knows each of us by name encourages us to recognize our true worth as individuals. Knowing and using someone's name is the first step to relationship with that person. And God is a relational God. Throughout the Bible we see evidence of God's dealings with individuals. He frequently used their personal names as a means of introducing Himself to them.

One great leader of the Children of Israel first heard God use his name when he was a nobody. A rejected, runaway Egyptian prince of Hebrew slave descent, he found himself working as a shepherd, looking after someone else's sheep in the back end of nowhere. Hardly a top achiever! Instead he was a lonely man, with a speech impediment and only smelly sheep for company. There must have been times when he felt that he had messed up his life-chances completely.

But neither previous failure nor desolate location eclipses us from God's radar. God loved this man, who would eventually become known as "the friend of God" (Isaiah 41:8; James 2:23), and He used unusual circumstances to get his attention. Just the way He does with us sometimes.

"Moses, Moses!" God called to the shepherd, who had turned aside to watch a bush burn, while remaining intact.

When Moses replied to the Voice that somehow knew his name, he simply said: "Here I am."

Only after God had declared Himself as the God of his ancestors, Abraham, Isaac and Jacob, did Moses realize Whose presence he was in, and subsequently he responded with due reverence (Exodus 3:1–6).

From this point on, the insignificant failure became a man of great character and faith, because he knew that God would be with him, whatever lay ahead. And, my word, there were some difficult journeys ahead for Moses! But he was to learn, little by little, to trust deeply in the God who knew his name.

Centuries later, a man of short stature, much despised by his own community, also heard God call his name. On this occasion it was the Son of God who spoke, and the fact that Jesus was actually speaking to the likes of him drew much criticism to the Saviour. But Jesus didn't care what others said, because this man was just as important to Him as anyone else.

"Zacchaeus," Jesus called to the man perched in the sycamore tree, "make haste and come down, for today I must stay at your house" (Luke 19:5).

I'm sure Zacchaeus almost fell out of the tree when he heard the miracle-working rabbi from Nazareth call his name! I mean, no one ever wanted to visit with Zacchaeus – and the names they usually called him were unrepeatable! He had spent his life working as a tax collector for the hated Roman Empire, and was despised for it. He further lined his own pockets with what he stole in illegal additions to the taxes. He had only come that day to see who Jesus was, and had hoped that no one had watched him climb into the tree, so that he could actually see what was going on.

When Zacchaeus heard the Saviour call for *him*, the last thing on his mind was embarrassment.

For once in his life he was being treated like a human being, and for once in his life he did what was right. In the presence of Jesus, Zacchaeus didn't need to be reminded that he was a sinner; he was only too aware of it. In willing repentance, his life was forever changed, and through restitution his actions declared what had just happened in his heart.

Recognizing true penitence in this little man from Jericho, Jesus went on to declare to the watching crowds: "Today salvation has come to this house ... for the Son of Man has come to seek and to save that which was lost" (Luke 19:9–10).

And it all started with the calling of a name, which in turn made a person of disreputable character realize that he was looked on by God as important – and loved in spite of himself.

Moses and Zacchaeus are just two examples that show how important we are to God. We do not – neither could we – gain recognition with God by what we may or may not achieve in our own strength. In fact, the converse is true, if we believe the words of Jesus in Matthew 16:26: "And how do you benefit if you gain the whole world but lose your own soul in the process?" (NLT).

Instead it is wonderfully enriching to know that everybody is "somebody" in God's eyes. From the refugee camps on the Thailand–Burma border to the deserts of the Horn of Africa, from the jungle tribes of South America to the prison camps of North Korea, from the exclusive streets of Paris to the ghettoes of New York, from the remote farms of the Northern Territories to the high-rise buildings of Hong Kong – each one of us is seen by God as an individual of great worth and eternal significance.

So, how does God see me?

He sees me as one whom He has created: "Have we not all one Father? Has not one God created us?" (Malachi 2:10).

He sees me as His child, to protect and care for: "You see me when I travel and when I rest at home … You place your hand of blessing on my head" (Psalm 139:3, 5 NLT).

He sees me as a person upon whom He has set His affection: "For God so loved the world that he gave his one and only Son, that whoever believes in him shall not perish but have eternal life" (John 3:16 NIV).

He sees me as sinful, yet worth sending His Son to die for: "But God demonstrates His own love toward us, in that while we were still sinners, Christ died for us" (Romans 5:8).

He sees me as an individual for whom He has great plans: "'I know the plans I have for you,' says the LORD. 'They are plans for good and not for disaster, to give you a future and a hope'" (Jeremiah 29:11 NLT).

How does God see me?

How does God see me?

He sees me as any loving and devoted Father sees his own child: someone to love, protect, teach, guide and sacrifice for. He is not harsh or unloving, as some fathers have been towards their children, for God's love goes further than we can ever imagine.

And it is from this premise that we must start when suffering touches our lives. In the days when our human response is to wonder if God cares for us, we will find the route to the answer shorter with this realization firmly fixed in our minds: *We matter to God!*

The question of fairness

The page was full of colour.

A ball of yellow filled one corner, while thick streaks emanated from the mass, mimicking the sun's bright rays. Brightly coloured flowers reached halfway up the front of a redbrick house. A happy picture was emerging, drawn by a very happy almost-four-year-old boy. Our son was working carefully on the picture that would soon adorn a kitchen cupboard in his grandmother's house. The sound of humming filled the room as he continued with his masterpiece.

I was looking on quietly as I fed the latest addition to our family, totally unprepared for what came next.

Without so much as lifting his head, he started to speak: "Mummy?" he said, pausing for a second.

Recognizing a question was coming, I replied with a simple "Yes, son? What is it?"

He reached into the old biscuit tin for another crayon. "Mummy, is Joy handicapped too – like Cheryl?"

Panic filled my heart. Thoughts raced through my mind as I tried to fight back the tears that were suddenly stinging my eyes. We had wanted to protect our lovely son from this; wanted to wait a while before we told him the dreadful news that his daddy and I were having difficulty coming to terms with. I tried to keep my composure as he simply worked on at his drawing, but my heart was shouting out to God, pleading for help.

I was afraid that my answer would disappoint Paul. He had looked forward to the new baby coming with such enthusiasm, and it didn't bother him one bit when the baby turned out to be another girl. The picture of his little face on the first day he saw her filled my mind as I tried to think what to say.

"Oh, God, please help me," I silently prayed. *"I don't know what to say. I don't want to hurt him. It's not fair, Lord!"*

"Is she, Mummy?"

This time Paul lifted his head and looked straight at me, surprised to see a tear fall down my face.

"Would you still love her, Paul, if she was like Cheryl?"

I knew how stupid the question was as soon as I asked it. I simply didn't know the right words to use. Anyway, small boys shouldn't know the word "handicapped".

"Don't be silly, Mummy!" he replied, running over to give us both a cuddle. "Of course I love her – she's my sister!"

"Well, Paul," I stammered, "Joy is handicapped – just like Cheryl."

He stroked Joy's little head and planted a sloppy kiss on her cheek.

"I love you, Joy," he whispered quietly in her ear before returning, totally unperturbed, to the floor to finish his picture.

Thirteen years later, on the night of Joy's death, he would say the words, "That's not fair!" for himself. And as a young man Paul would have to struggle with God for answers to the question of fairness in his own mind and heart. But for now, it was OK.

I wish I could say it was the same for me.

Joy's diagnosis had sent me to a very dark place.

It was the unfairness of it all that took its toll. The disappointment that God would do this to us again was overwhelming. I could not understand why He would allow lightning, as it were, to strike twice in our lives – and with such devastating consequences.

Cheryl was five years old, and Paul almost three, when my husband and I decided to try for another baby. A paediatrician had let it slip that it was rare for children with Cheryl's condition to reach their teens. We knew only too well that she was profoundly disabled but, until that time, had never considered that one day she would die. Apart from the effect that would have on us, we were deeply saddened to think that Paul would be left as an only child. He was such a sociable boy. We wanted him to have a sibling whom he could grow up with. A brother or sister who he could talk to, sharing his dreams, his jokes – and maybe even his secrets.

So I became pregnant, confident that God saw our motivation in taking this risk, and convinced that the odds of 1:8 at best and 1:4 at worst of another child with microcephaly were in our favour.

I kept well throughout my pregnancy and we were all excited at the prospect of another baby. Added to all this, we had literally hundreds of people praying for us. What could go wrong?

"Home in a boat, Mrs Campbell!" the obstetrician said, a huge grin parting his face. "Nothing wrong with this baby – this one's perfect!"

As I left the antenatal clinic that day, my feet didn't touch the floor. I was ecstatic! Never could there have been a greater contrast between two pronouncements over two children than there was over Cheryl and my unborn child. On the one hand, the words: "She will never be normal!" And on the other: "This one's perfect!"

The praise in our hearts, and from others across the world, was overflowing. God had heard our prayer. We would have another healthy child, and Paul, even though he loved Cheryl dearly, would now have a brother or sister who could actually play with him!

The weeks leading up to my delivery passed in a haze of excitement; God's peace was my daily companion, in spite of the usual discomfort of late pregnancy.

"It's a girl!" was the announcement from the midwife.

While I was pregnant Philip and I had had no preference over the sex of our baby. Our only concern was that he or she would be well and healthy. With that concern put to rest a few weeks earlier, we were now both especially delighted that it was a girl.

As her proud daddy held her in his arms for the first time, he voiced the words that were already in my heart: "God has given us a perfect daughter, Catherine. We have to call her Joy. There's no other name we can give her!"

I had to agree.

In the hours and days that followed *joy* burst from our lives. We wore permanent grins. Everyone who heard about her or saw her was full of *joy* – especially her big brother! Even Cheryl smiled when we wrapped her arms around the wriggly, noisy little bundle we brought home that July day.

Yet as the weeks wore on, the little niggle I had had in the hospital started to disturb me. Then, I had commented on how Joy looked so like Cheryl. Responses about sisters looking alike did nothing to settle me. It was Joy's head that bothered me. It was small, like Cheryl's – and I was afraid. Unwilling to allow my "silly" concerns to cause anxiety in the family, I had arranged to take Joy to see the paediatrician who cared for Cheryl. Unfortunately I had to go alone that morning, as Cheryl was sick and Philip had to stay home with her. That didn't matter, I had told myself; it was just to put all these worries to rest. No one else need ever know.

But soon everyone would have to know, because during this particular hospital visit the word "perfect" was not used.

"I'm sorry," the paediatrician said.

Her words floored me: I didn't want her to continue. I wanted to stop her; to run away before she could finish what I now knew she was going to say. But my body wasn't quick enough … I couldn't move.

"I'm sorry … Joy's brain has stopped growing. She has the same condition as Cheryl."

I looked at her in horror, her words feeling like blows from a baseball bat. Maybe it would have been better if she had hit me – at least I could recover from that.

But not this! How could I recover from this?

And as I looked at our beautiful little Joy, asleep in my arms, I knew exactly what this would mean.

Only six weeks old, but condemned to a life in which she would never walk or talk, sing or see. Condemned to a life tormented by seizures, muscle disorders, feeding problems and chest infections.

Heading for home, I had no idea how I would tell my big-hearted husband that his darling Joy had microcephaly, hating the fact that I had been right all along, that my "silly" worries had come true with nightmarish accuracy. How would we tell Paul that the first person he ran to see when he came home from nursery school every day would never ride his bike or build Lego with him? How would we tell our families and friends that we were wrong, that God had not answered our many prayers, as we had first thought?

I have no memory of the journey home that day – only of the words that kept bouncing back off the windscreen at me: "That's not fair, Lord! That's just not fair!"

To travel along the same road twice had not been in my plan, and I was intensely disappointed that God had not agreed. The sense of unfairness was suffocating.

You see, I had had six years with Cheryl by this stage. Six amazing years. Yes, there was heartache, but they were also years when my relationship with God was taken to an altogether different level. Daily I was learning the truth behind the words of 2 Samuel 22:31: "As for God, His way is perfect". I had come to realize that Cheryl was no freak of nature, nor merely the product of faulty genes: God's view of perfection was very different to that of our day and society.

Psalm 139 had become a revelation of gargantuan proportions to me, transforming my thinking about disability and disease:

You made all the delicate, inner parts of my body
and knit me together in my mother's womb ...
You watched me as I was being formed in utter seclusion,
as I was woven together in the dark of the womb.
You saw me before I was born.
Every day of my life was recorded ...
before a single day had passed.

PSALM 139:13, 15–16 NLT

These verses speak of a God who knows exactly how those He has created will turn out. Every bone formed in secret, every vessel, every nerve; the delicate, intricate workings of what makes us human – He has watched it all come together, and knows exactly how each one of us will fit perfectly into His plan – even if the original design has been left flawed by the fall. How comforting it is to know that God has even numbered our days before the first one begins. Neither our lives nor our deaths are a surprise to Him.

Psalm 139 proved to me that life is not some form of cosmic lottery: God has His purposes and plans and we are at the very centre of them.

As far as Cheryl was concerned, the medical profession could not "fix" what they saw as a broken child, but God's plans for using her were by now becoming evident, as the story of her life was already encouraging and blessing others. Cheryl was undoubtedly a person of worth and eternal significance.

In those years I had also experienced the peace of God in a way that was as real as the rain or the sunshine that touched my face. And as I delved into the Bible, looking for more and more answers to the myriad of questions that our family's suffering threw up, I discovered that God doesn't only make promises – He keeps them.

I had been taught so much up to this point, but there was pain in the learning ... and I didn't want to learn any more. I'd had enough.

Having discovered that Cheryl was no mistake, I should have been able to follow through with the same reasoning: Joy too was no mistake – God had a plan for her life as well. But I didn't want to think that way. Acceptance involved too much pain for all of us. Instead I chose anger at the seeming unfairness of it all.

It just wasn't fair!

Yet I could not get away from what God had already done in my heart, or the evidence I had built up over the previous six years of God's love for me. He had promised to be with me, and He had kept His word. I had not been abandoned ... but I was angry with God. However, I also knew that if I would take time to listen, He would speak into my situation.

Of all the lessons I have learnt through pain, the biggest has probably been that God is a speaking God – and He speaks through His Word, the Bible.

So day by day I would read a devotional book called *Streams in the Desert* written by Mrs Charles E. Cowman,[1] and ask God to speak to me. And on one day God spoke to my broken, angry heart.

I read of a conversation about how china tableware is fired. A customer had noticed that the design was much clearer on one set than another. She enquired as to how that happened and was told: "This had to be put through the fire a second time to get the design on it." The pattern, it seems, only becomes clear after the second firing.

And as I read and reread the story, I heard God's tender voice asking me to trust Him – to trust Him with the things that I didn't understand at the time. I could hear Him remind me that there was more going on than I could see – a much bigger picture – and that He would eventually produce something beautiful, just like the china. The path of my pain was going full circle, coming back once more to recognizing the big, eternal picture and to taking the step of accepting faith.

"Faith" – a small word and often misused.

The acrostic of FAITH – Forsaking All, I Trust Him – sounds so amiable, so easy. But I have discovered that faith is not easy – it is hard! For there are times when God asks us to come to the edge with Him – to a painful place, to a lonely place, even to a cruel and unfair place. Once there, He asks us to step out into the seeming void with Him. That's what faith is: trusting God when we don't know what lies ahead, when we can't understand the plan He wants us to be part of.

The sentence at the end of that devotional thought invited me to take another step of faith: "Don't rebel at the second breath of the flame, if He sends it," it said.

And God asked me one more time: "Can you trust Me, Catherine, with the things that you don't understand?"

"Yes, Lord," I replied, as I stepped off the edge once more with my Heavenly Father.

And in response to that step of faith, peace once more returned to my wounded heart.

We all struggle at times with the question of fairness. Humanly speaking, there is much that is unfair about this world. Children starve; women are brutalized; Christians are tortured; unjust governments steal from their own poor; cancer takes a loved one; infidelity breaks up a home. The list appears endless.

Even Habakkuk became incensed at God's apparent unfairness when He answered the prophet's prayer for heavenly intervention by the threat of foreign invasion! You can almost hear the prophet shout, "That's not fair, Lord!" in his response to God in Habakkuk chapter 1. But as Habakkuk took time to be alone with God (2:1) and to listen to what He had to say, the prophet began his journey towards acceptance. That journey took Habakkuk down memory lane as he reminded himself of all that God had done for Israel in their very shaky past.

After all of his deliberations, Habakkuk came to the conclusion that God had never let His people down to this point, and so he willingly accepted whatever lay ahead and was prepared to trust God – even though he didn't fully understand what God was doing. Habakkuk was aware that God always had a bigger picture in mind.

The prophet's beautiful acceptance speech is recorded in Habakkuk 3:17–18:

Though the fig tree may not blossom,
Nor fruit be on the vines;
Though the labor of the olive may fail,
And the fields yield no food;
Though the flock may be cut off from the fold,
And there be no herd in the stalls –
Yet I will rejoice in the LORD,
I will joy in the God of my salvation.

Perhaps we would do well to follow the old prophet's example. It is easy to allow our disappointment to become a tool that locks away our memories of all that God has done for us in the past. Yet those very memories will help us to see that God is for us, and only ever acts for good on our behalf.

With God it is not a question of fairness but of trust. The more important question for us is therefore: Are we prepared to trust God – even with the things that we don't understand?

When angels come to call

"Actions speak louder than words." Or so the old adage goes.

In many situations words are enough. Concern that is voiced can encourage or bring comfort; apologies that are sincerely spoken can lead to healing; love that is declared strengthens the bond. Words are undoubtedly a vital component of meaningful communication. There are also times in many strong, long-term relationships when those who are close can enjoy each other's company in periods of silence, as much as with words. However, non-verbal communication has its limitations. Where appropriate, it is always better to use words.

We need to hear words – especially those that affirm, encourage, give direction, and tell us we are loved. As human beings, we differ from our animal counterparts in many ways, but language in particular makes us stand out distinctly from all the rest. We were born with the ability to communicate verbally with intelligence and specificity, which in turn allows us to live complicated and intricate lives. We were also made in the image of God (Genesis 1:27), and as God has always demonstrated His desire to communicate with us by the use of words, so we have that ability to do the same with others and with our Creator.

Words matter!

Words can build up.

A simple "thank you" can make your day. A compliment given

at just the right moment can make you feel special. A term of endearment can lift your heart. Even someone remembering your name can boost your spirits.

But words can also tear us down.

A thoughtless comment, an unfair rebuke, an unkind remark, gossip, an angry statement, a declaration of hatred – each can leave its damaging mark on our lives.

Therefore, "Better to say nothing!" is the excuse some would make for shallow interactions with others. "Don't apologize, it only attributes blame," they reason. "Don't say thank you for work well done," as it may look like you have favourites. "Don't say 'I love you'," that's too emotional.

But "nothing" is simply that – nothing! And where there is a void, people tend to fill it, often with their own perception of what you are not saying!

Words are important.

The offices of marriage guidance counsellors resound with: "He hasn't told me that he loves me for years!" The usual reply is: "You know I love you – I don't need to tell you!" Or: "I didn't know you felt that way – why didn't you tell me?"

Silence can be damaging.

Undoubtedly, we are all different, each of us requiring varying levels of affirmation and communication, yet all needing to hear that we are on someone's heart – especially when we are going through a rough patch.

At times, words are enough. At other times, words need to be backed by action – that visible confirmation that what we say or think is actually true. Action is the tangible proof, if you like, that someone really cares about us, and what we are going through.

Consequently, in very many cases actions do speak louder than words. And that is also true of God. The Bible is literally full of the verbal evidence that God cares for us. Those words are now available to us in written form, as God is not afraid to use words. Alongside these verbal proofs of God's love for His children is recorded the historical evidence of how He has acted for our benefit in the past, to show us how much He really cares for us as individuals.

Elijah is a case in point.

The silence was broken by the bleating of the goats whose place of shelter had been usurped by the old man. The sun was high in the sky, lizards retreating beneath the craggy rocks of the Negev, while Yahweh's prophet collapsed under the shadow cast by the broom tree.

Barely able to keep his eyes open, Elijah was thankful for the cover of the desert shrub. Its small leaves and thin, wispy branches provided the weary traveller with layers of shade, cooling his hot skin in the desolate area of wilderness in which he now found himself. His low mood prevented the pleasurable smell of the shrub's delicate flowers from registering in his tired brain. Now situated about a hundred miles south of where his journey had started, Elijah's problems were made worse by exhaustion and dehydration. The rain he had left behind in Jezreel would have been welcome here, in this barren place of the past wanderings of the Children of Israel.

But Elijah didn't care!

Drought and rain had to do with past battles, and Elijah's problem was that he had forgotten that they were battles he had *won*. With God's help he had been the victor. Under God's direction he had defeated Baal-merqart, the so-called protector of Tyre. With his own eyes, he had watched the humiliation and defeat of this incapable "god" of stone. Better still, he had heard Israel declare once more that "The LORD, He is God! The LORD, He is God!" when the fire fell from Heaven, completely consuming the sacrifice on the altar on that day of all days on Mount Carmel.

Yet, sitting under the broom tree, Elijah's memories of the miraculous seemed to be hidden away behind a wall of fear, which was cemented together by an overwhelming weariness of both body and soul. He could no longer bring to mind the sight of the ravens bringing him food by Cherith Brook, or the years he had safely spent in Zarephath in the home of the widow, while Jezebel's soldiers scoured the country looking for him. Even the laughter of the young boy raised to life again couldn't pull Elijah back to what was reality – that Yahweh was undefeated and His prophet was safe and secure.

This faithful, normally fearless, prophet of God was totally burnt out: misery was now his only companion. His sense of failure – caused by running away from the threats of an evil pagan queen – overcame his knowledge of the Holy One, while circumstances, situations and physical limitations had sent him spiralling downwards into despair.

Yet, perhaps coming to this place was about more than running away. For Yahweh's prophet knew that it was through this desert place that he must travel in order to reach Horeb, the Mountain of God. But by the time Elijah had reached the broom tree he could go no further.

He had had all he could take!

"And he prayed that he might die, and said: 'It is enough! Now, LORD, take my life, for I am no better than my fathers!'" (1 Kings 19:4).

No sooner had the cry of desperation left his lips than a comforting blanket of sleep caressed Elijah's weary frame. Yahweh was near at hand … and He knew just what His servant needed. The darkness now overtaking Elijah was not that of the death he had requested, but of energy-giving sleep.

Elijah had no idea how long he had been asleep.

Suddenly, he felt a gentle shake ... someone touching him! Startled for a second, knowing that the only visitors to this wilderness location were mountain goats and wild beasts, Elijah stiffened as he was further roused by a voice.

"Arise and eat," were the words that finally brought him to wakefulness.

He sat up, looking around for the source of the voice he had heard so clearly. As he rubbed his eyes, all he could see were some bugs scurrying for cover. The only noise piercing his ears was the squawking of the scavenging birds overhead.

He must have been dreaming.

Or that was what he thought, until the aroma of freshly baked bread filled his nostrils! And there, positioned beside the weary prophet's head, was breakfast! A whole cake of bread sitting waiting for him on the hot coals, and a jar of cold, thirst-quenching water alongside it!

As Elijah broke off a piece of the hot bread, he didn't need to ask where it had come from. Yahweh had provided for him before – that much he remembered. God must have sent His angel, Elijah concluded, drinking from the jar as he had once drunk from the brook when Yahweh had told him to flee from Ahab the first time.

"But God didn't tell me to run this time – I did that all by myself!"

Pronouncements of failure only caused the dark clouds of depression to settle around Elijah yet again. Nevertheless, the tormenting thoughts were quickly banished, as heavy eyes now accompanied the comforting feeling of a full stomach. He was experiencing the reality of what King David had said in Psalm 127:2, "He gives His beloved sleep", even though he was unaware of it at the time.

And the beasts of both land and air did not dare to come near what would normally have been an easy meal for them. Not with angels about!

Some time later, Elijah was wakened again. He felt someone touch him for a second time. Only this time, he was more alert: this time he was not only better rested but also more aware of what was going on. Yet there was something about this touch that was different from the first. This touch was divine! This touch felt as though God Himself had put His hand not only on Elijah's broken body, but on his wounded heart.

Elijah recognized that this angel was no mere messenger from God, but the Angel of the Lord Himself.

On that day, God was visiting the desert: a desert not merely of geographical location, but also the desert of Elijah's soul.

"Arise and eat," the Voice said once more, following this simple command with a merciful statement of deep understanding: "because the journey is too great for you."

Through the second person of the Trinity, known as the Angel of the Lord in Old Testament times, Yahweh was confirming to His despairing prophet that He understood his frailty, and recognized that Elijah still had a long and difficult journey ahead of him.

So instead of rebuke for unbelief and fear, the Lord God sent physical evidence of His unfailing love to a weary and discouraged man. And both the sleep and sustenance provided by those ministering angels allowed Elijah to continue his long, difficult journey to meet with God on Mount Horeb.

God's actions spoke louder than His words would have been able to in Elijah's wilderness experience.

I find in this amazing story of the tenderness of God, recorded in 1 Kings 19, all the evidence I will ever need that God shows His compassion in tangible ways to His hurting children. The words used by the Angel of the Lord in verse 7 tear at my heart. Just imagine – the Lord knew that "the journey was too great" for His faithful servant. He didn't stand idly by while Elijah suffered. He did something about it – something wonderful!

Commentators, preachers and individuals throughout the ages have often delivered their interpretation on these verses with harshness, concentrating on the runaway prophet who had let God down. Perhaps, even today, we are too quick to judge the failures of others, and of ourselves, with the wagging-finger approach.

Of course Elijah should have known better; of course he shouldn't have run away; of course he shouldn't have moved out of God's plan for his life. But, thankfully, God is a God of mercy, who rarely treats us as we deserve – and I am so glad! For God not only knows how we are feeling but also what we need, and reaches out to us with a Father's understanding, ministering to us in love.

And for that to happen, He often sends "angels" to call.

A volunteer for "onion duty" was not something the cook often received. Conscription was usually required! But standing in line that summer morning in the kitchen of a Christian Holiday Centre, volunteer was exactly what I did.

"Sorry," the cook grimaced as she looked apologetically at her kitchen helpers, "but I need a whole sack of onions peeled and chopped this morning. Any volunteers?"

"I'll do it!" I shouted back at her, before the request had barely left her lips.

"Are you sure, Catherine? It's an awful job – I thought maybe one of the guys could do it."

"No, please – I want to do it!"

Sensing an almost pleading tone to my reply, the cook agreed, and I made a quick retreat to the tiny food-preparation room behind the main kitchen before she had even allocated duties to the rest of the team.

I sighed as the knife in my hand made a sharp cut into the first of a great many onions. This was the perfect place for me today. No one ever came in here – I felt securely alone. It was just the way I wanted it. The reality of what had taken place on the previous day was sinking in: I couldn't face the public today. And if I cried, I would have the onions to blame!

Yet, on the face of it, Cheryl's first birthday celebration had gone very well.

Both staff and residents of the Christian camp had made such a fuss of her, and she dutifully smiled back at each one. The young members of staff had clubbed together and presented her with a teddy bear that was almost as big as she was! They little understood how far independent play was from Cheryl's capabilities. And the cake that the cook had baked was huge – but Cheryl couldn't eat cake.

We had brought her beautiful birthday dress away with us – pink-print cotton with a sculptured lace collar, and tied in a gorgeous bow at the back. Her wavy, blonde hair set off her lightly tanned skin, surrounding those baby-blue eyes.

She looked absolutely beautiful!

"First birthdays are meant to be special!" I complained to the growing mound of chopped, smelly vegetables, my nose already starting to drip with the fumes.

"First birthdays are meant to be joyful occasions!" my complaining continued.

"Teddy bears! Cake! Cards!" By now, the knife was moving at speed, and I knew if I wasn't more careful I might soon be looking for plasters. "What do they know about Cheryl's birthday? What do they know about what it really means?"

As I reached for the enormous pot that was to be the recipient of my tearful work, I could hear the words of the paediatrician ringing in my ears.

"If Cheryl cannot sit up unaided by her first birthday, then there is a big question over her physical development."

"Well, she can't sit up by herself," I continued, talking to myself. "In fact she can't even hold her own head up! Now what does that mean, Dr Clever-Clogs?"

The paediatrician wasn't in the tiny room to answer my question. What was worse, though, was that I knew exactly what the answer was.

Cheryl was not going to be one of those whom I considered to be the "lucky" ones; those whose microcephaly caused only mild learning difficulties. She was now at the far end of the spectrum, suffering from severe physical and learning difficulties.

Her first birthday had proved it.

Sitting up all by herself was beyond her.

And as I walked through my wilderness of despair, I felt like pushing Elijah sideways to enable me to share the shade of his broom tree. The journey ahead was looking too difficult. I had had enough! But God was present in my desert, exactly as He had been in Elijah's. I simply didn't recognize His presence at that time.

"Can I help?"

The realization that someone else was in the room startled me. Without turning to see who it was, I curtly replied, "No thanks, I'm fine."

"Are you crying?" the intruder inquired.

"Well, that's a silly question!" I quipped. "I'm chopping onions, you know – hundreds of them!"

By now, I was becoming fraught, unhappy with the intrusion, unable to get rid of my unwelcome visitor.

"I've seen people cry over onions before – it's the sobbing and heaving shoulders that are puzzling me."

My cover had been blown! Now I was trapped in a small room with a man I barely knew, who wanted to sympathize. It was more than I could bear.

"Would you like to talk about it?" he persisted, blocking my way of escape with his tall, gangly frame. "I'm a good listener."

"You wouldn't understand!" I yelled – but he did.

This man, who was prepared to stand and listen to me wailing through my disappointments over Cheryl's secret birthday failings, had himself buried four out of his six premature babies. He knew what the wilderness was like. He had also sat under the broom tree.

He made very few comments on my litany of disaster, but before letting me escape the onion-hell I had volunteered for, he said something simple, yet profound.

"It's OK to cry, Catherine – just don't shut God out."

But my wall of fear about the future was cemented by a weariness of both body and soul.

A few days later I was about to take Cheryl to our room for her afternoon nap when I was ambushed in the hallway by some of the other staff wives. One of them took Cheryl's buggy from my hands, while another firmly gripped my elbow, leading me in the direction of the main door of the old building. The third conspirator took my room key and announced their intentions.

"We have decided that you need to get away from here for a little while. We will look after Cheryl – you are going with Anne."

I tried to protest, but it was to no avail. Soon I was sitting in a hair salon in the nearby town, being treated to a new hairstyle! That was followed by an afternoon cream tea in a beautiful English tea-room, replete with lace curtains and fine bone china. Little posies of flowers fragranced the genteel room, and it wasn't long before I heard myself laugh – something that had been missing for a long time.

On the return journey I wondered how these ladies could possibly have afforded to treat me to such luxury. Like me, two of their number struggled financially on the low salary of our evangelist husbands. I was deeply touched by their thoughtfulness, unaware that there was even more to come.

Arriving back at my room, I was met with a huge pile of laundry sitting on my bed – each item had been lovingly ironed and folded by the busiest woman in the Christian Holiday Centre. To this day I do not know what she had had to cancel to become a maid for the afternoon!

I sat on the bed – crying again – only this time I was overwhelmed by the expressions of love that had been shown to this sad, tired, young mother. And as I sat alone with my thoughts, I could hear God whisper in my ear:

"Catherine – I know – I know that the journey is too great for you."

"And so You sent Your ministering 'angels', Lord," I replied.

"Yes. Sometimes actions speak louder than words."

Often throughout the twenty years that I cared for either, or both, of our precious daughters, I have been very aware of the touch of God through those He has lovingly sent into my life. They have been the physical expression of the love of God to me on both the darkest of days, and on those days when I have been just plain tired.

They have been my ministering "angels" – those who have come to deliver a message of love and understanding from God to my soul. These "angels" have come in all shapes and sizes – some known to me, others strangers. Their method of delivery has also been diverse. Some filled my table with food when I couldn't think straight enough to shop, while others cleaned or ironed or babysat. For many of them, their delivery from God only took a few minutes – they didn't wish to intrude; while others sat into the long dark hours of the night to keep me company beside a hospital bed. Some prayed when I could no longer find the words;

others called with a hug, or a flower, or a card, or a message left on the phone. One even tended a grave for me when I went away for the first time following Cheryl's death.

And I have discovered that when "angels" come to call, an invisible tag is attached to each one of their gifts, with words from 1 Kings 19:7 inscribed by an understanding God:

"Catherine, I know that the journey is too great for you."

And I am eternally grateful for the expressions of such love.

But what would have happened if Elijah had not accepted the ministry of the angels that God had sent into the desert on those two occasions? What if he had left the cake of bread untouched or the water had remained in the jar? What if the depressed prophet had refused to listen to the words spoken by the angels? What if the expressions of God's care and concern had been refused?

The answers to those questions don't bear thinking about. Our final memory of Elijah might have been so different – one of failure and despair, rather than of further usefulness in the plan of God. Would we have read of a miserable death in a desert place, rather than the final victorious chariot ride of a faithful prophet through the whirlwind? Would someone other than Elijah have had to be chosen to stand with Moses and Jesus on the Mount of Transfiguration?

Thankfully, these are questions we do not need to consider, because Elijah was prepared to accept the help that God sent his way.

Unfortunately, we are not always so wise, sometimes allowing pride to turn from our door the very help that God sends to us. How often have the words "I'm managing fine, thank you," left our lips when a kind offer of assistance has come our way? Our experience of illness or heartache could be so different if we are willing to accept help. To know that another person is willing to draw alongside is deeply humbling, in the right sense of the word, and can make the burden we are carrying so much lighter. Accepting a tangible expression of love and care can also help to blow away the black clouds that often threaten when our lives are besieged by pain and stress.

Like Elijah, the end of our story can be completely different if we are prepared to welcome the "angels" who come to call.

Do I care?

Have you ever had a mouth ulcer?

It's a pesky little thing! So tiny that it's barely visible, yet not so small that you can't feel it. Then as soon as you put food into your mouth it feels as though it has suddenly grown to twice its original size. It's hard to believe that something so small can be so irritating. In fact, the annoyance it causes can affect your whole body; it can make you feel miserable. Before too long you need to get your finger into your mouth to apply some soothing gel.

Or what about a little splinter that has embedded itself in your toe? Ouch! You can feel the pain just thinking about it, can't you? Every step you take is excruciating – until you discover the exact spot where the little trouble-maker went in, and with tweezers in hand, you fish it out!

No matter how minor the ailment, or how specific the location of the problem, we need to use other parts of our body to help ease the pain.

But what happens when something really major goes wrong with our bodies? The physical response within the body is unbelievable. We have been created with the ability to react in a myriad of different ways at one time in order to facilitate survival. Help literally rushes to the affected areas of our bodies within milliseconds.

The brain receives the sensory messages telling it that something is wrong, via nerve impulses at speeds that can barely be measured. Forty-five miles of nerve fibres transport vital information back and forth to the brain and then on to every part of the body. Adrenaline and other biochemical reactions are instantly triggered to stimulate a variety of essential responses. The heart rate is increased to pump the blood faster to where it is needed, which in turn delivers the extra glucose and oxygen required during the trauma. Meanwhile the blood supply to the peripheries is shut down temporarily, to ensure that the vital organs are served first.

Excruciating pain is dulled by the release of increased levels of endorphins – just to help you survive the initial assault on your system. And all the while, platelets and fibrin are rushing to block the holes in your blood vessels with blood clots, to stop you bleeding to death.

Who would deny that we are indeed "fearfully and wonderfully made" (Psalm 139:14)? Yet each individual part of these amazing bodies of ours is pretty useless on its own. Each part and each system needs the others to function effectively, each relying on the others to come to its rescue in times of trauma and disease. Therefore each part is important.

The apostle Paul reminds us in 1 Corinthians 12:21–22 that: "the eye cannot say to the hand, 'I have no need of you'; nor again the head to the feet, 'I have no need of you'… those members of the body which seem to be weaker are necessary."

Just as the different parts of the body need the others, "so we, being many, are one body in Christ" (Romans 12:5) and we "ought to love one another" (1 John 4:11).

As individuals we should not only be aware of the suffering of other brothers and sisters in Christ, but share in it with them (1 Corinthians 12:26). The apostle Paul encouraged the individual members of the suffering church in Galatia to "Share each other's burdens, and in this way obey the law of Christ" (Galatians 6:2

NLT). How precious it must have been to those early disciples to receive the support of others when life became unbearable: to know that they were not alone in their pain.

That same experience is ours when someone takes the time to draw alongside us. As part of Christ's body, we are God's hands and feet, the tools He can use to help those who need to see God's words turned into action.

We can become God's "angels", bringing tangible messages that speak of hope and love and comfort.

Once we come to grips with how God sees us, and the lengths to which He goes to demonstrate His love, the question, "Does God care?" becomes irrelevant, because God's actions have long since spoken louder than His words.

The question, however, is then turned around.

Do we care?

Do we care enough about the suffering of others to respond with the same love and care that is often shown to us, or which we would like to receive if our underlying fault line shook today?

Are we prepared to be the hands used to deliver a token of God's love to the lonely? Didn't Jesus Himself say: "if you give even a cup of cold water to one of the least of my followers, you will surely be rewarded" (Matthew 10:42 NLT)? A bowl of soup may not hold much monetary value, but in indicating that we care, it is of enormous value.

Will we allow our feet to walk into the life of someone who has been deserted or abused, involving ourselves in situations that take longer than the delivery of a bowl of soup?

Are we willing to take the time to "weep with those who weep" (Romans 12:15)? Shoulder-lending brings such comfort! Can we brighten a sad home with flowers, or touch a hurting heart with some sentiment on a card? Does a hug need to be given, or an encouraging word spoken? Will a bowl be filled with food in

Africa today because of a decision we made? Or will a persecuted pastor in a far-off land be released because we took a few seconds to sign a petition? Because, I can assure you, that with each act of kindness that we give in Jesus' name, there is an invisible card attached.

"*I know*," the recipient will read, "*I know that the journey is too great for you.*"

And as they hold in their hands, or experience in their lives, the concern of another human being, they feel the loving touch of a Heavenly Father, who really does care.

Notes

1. Mrs Charles E. Cowman, *Streams in the Desert*, Vol. 3, Lakeland Marshall Pickering, 1985, pp. 330f.

Taking a closer look

- The fact that God knows us by name is both comforting and empowering. Meditate on Isaiah 43:1 and Exodus 33:17b today and recognize your significance to God.

- Read the story of Zacchaeus for yourself in Luke 19:1–10. In what way did Jesus treat this man differently? What does that say about how Jesus sees us?

- Humanly speaking, life frequently treats us unfairly. Read the book of Habakkuk – it's only three chapters long! Now work through the steps that Habakkuk took towards accepting what initially seemed so unfair.

- Is there something in your life that you feel is unfair? How will you come to the place of trusting God, in spite of your circumstances?

- Examine God's provision for Elijah up to the point of his "broom tree experience". The Brook Cherith: 1 Kings 17:1–7; lodging at Zarephath: 17:8–16; in the wilderness: 19:1–8. What can we learn from these stories?

- Read Acts 9:8–42. It contains the story of a little-known woman and the impact her acts of kindness had on her society. List what we can learn from the story of Dorcas.

FOUR

LOOKING AFTER YOUR SOUL

Weeding – dealing with bitterness

I don't like gardening.

No, that's not quite true. I strongly dislike gardening. Perhaps I should elaborate further – I hate gardening!

Don't get me wrong, I love to look at beautiful gardens; I even enjoy spending time walking through well-kept gardens, admiring their blooms and design. I also find the gardens of stately homes the perfect place to have a picnic. Just don't ask me to garden – I get a rash even thinking about it! My idea of purgatory is an afternoon at a garden centre – except for the ones with the lovely coffee shops and delicatessens. They are definitely worth a visit – but you won't see me leaving carrying plants in my arms.

You see, in my dictionary "gardening" is spelt "HARD WORK". And it's work that you have to keep going back to. It's never done! It rates along with ironing and window cleaning, except that it's right at the top of my "most hated chores" list. People try to tell me it's relaxing, yet even with our own low-maintenance garden, there is a love–hate relationship going on, especially with the weeds. They love me – I hate them!

My mother cannot understand where this aversion has come from. She, with a great deal of help from my father, has always kept her gardens looking lovely. I have even learnt the names of some shrubs and plants simply from walking around the garden in our family home. I love to see what they have been planting, and especially to smell the fragrance of the roses after it has been raining – something you don't get with the shop-bought varieties.

I am forever suggesting that perhaps my parents, now both in their eighties, should consider choosing plants that require less attention. Dead-heading, pruning and thinning (see – I do know some gardening terms!) all take time and energy which is in less supply as we grow older. The answer I receive, however, always runs along the same lines:

"You can't stop the weeds growing, Catherine," Mum replies, every time I bring the subject up. "Whatever is planted, you always have to deal with the weeds. And the sooner you deal with them, the easier they are to pull out."

I think she lives in hope that every little free piece of advice she gives might change my mind about gardening. However, I find her gardening information more spiritually enlightening than horticulturally challenging. Especially when she reminds me about what happens when you do nothing about the weeds:

"They can do so much damage if you leave them. Before long they take over the garden – and then you'll know what work really is!"

Come to think of it, I sense that Mum may have put her finger on where my aversion to gardening started. Our first house had a tiny front garden and, when we first moved in, I remember proudly digging out a little border around the edge. We couldn't afford for much of our limited resources to be spent on flowers and shrubs, so we started off sparingly, planting a few things here and there. Of course, that left too much bare soil – something the weeds simply loved! And so began a battle that I never succeeded in winning.

"Doing a bit of gardening?" my neighbour would say, as he looked over his ornate display of beautiful blooms to observe my annual bout of suffering.

"I'm giving it a bit of a go – again!" I would reply, feeling rather ashamed of my weed-infested border compared to his fragrant perfection.

"Keep up the good work!"

His encouraging words were genuinely meant, but they did sting a little as I considered my own obvious inadequacies, which were heavily accompanied by a desire to be doing something else. The kind man from next door would often return with the gift of a little seedling that he had nurtured, for me to add to my humble collection. Another piece of advice usually crowned our conversation. "You know, Catherine, if you would spend a few minutes in the garden every day, you'd be able to keep up with the weeds. It's not so much hard work then."

I think he must have been talking to my mum!

Whether I like gardening or not is pretty irrelevant, because I can appreciate the beauty and order that comes from those who are prepared to be involved in cultivation. Those who spend the time undoubtedly see the results. The gardeners who deal with the weeds quickly allow what is good in their garden the freedom to grow. I'm also aware that someone's garden can be affected by the weeds coming from neighbouring properties. Our weeds can be a nuisance to others.

This all reminds me that the Bible speaks of a weed that can grow in our lives. We neither plant it, nor want it. It seems to spring up all by itself, although generally in response to situations and circumstances that provide the perfect soil for its growth. Unfortunately, if we don't deal with it quickly and severely, it has the ability to cause havoc, affecting not only our own lives, but also the lives of those around us.

It will affect our Christian growth as it twists our perception and fills the place in our souls that should be given up to better things.

It will sap our strength, especially the energy we need to deal with the original situation that first allowed it in. As it grows in size, it will blot out the sunshine of God's comfort and peace, casting an even larger shadow of despair across our already damaged lives. And, sadly, it will affect our Christian testimony, as onlookers watch us display an unhelpful response to our pain. It may even creep in to the lives of others, widening its destructive cycle.

I am, of course, speaking of the "root of bitterness", and I have discovered that hurting hearts make fertile soil for this caustic weed. The writer to the Hebrews warns members of the early church about the damage it can do, and the speed at which it can spread. "See to it ..." he warns, "that no bitter root grows up to cause trouble and defile many" (Hebrews 12:15 NIV).

Which of us has not, at some time or another, been hurt by unkind words or thoughtless actions? Perhaps we may even go as far as to blame God for our heartache. Our anger appears justifiable, and our response seems rightly deserved. After all, we are the ones who are suffering! We reason that the one who has delivered our pain deserves to be punished with our resentment. Unfortunately, it isn't too long before that anger and resentment takes on an intensity that we find difficult to control. Bitterness towards the person concerned, or even towards God, soon winds itself around our soul.

Attitudes of forgiveness and acceptance are soon choked as the weed takes an obsessive hold of our lives. In time we become slaves to the negative impact that it has on us, forever pointing the finger of blame at someone else. We fail to see that our personal response to what has happened has severely added to our misery.

Perhaps there is no more telling example of this than what is recorded in the Old Testament book of Ruth. It introduces us to two women. Both of them have been dealt hard blows in life, yet they respond in completely different ways.

Naomi was a Hebrew woman who set up home in the neighbouring country of Moab, after she and her family left Bethlehem during a time of famine. At first, life seemed good to her, her husband and their two sons – but tragedy was not far away. She no longer had famine to deal with, but soon she was sadly widowed in that foreign land, and left with two sons. When both of them took local brides, Naomi settled once more. Mahlon, her eldest, married Ruth, while Chilion married Orpah.

Another ten years passed before disaster struck Naomi's life again. On this occasion it was also to affect both of her daughters-in-law greatly, when, horror of horrors ... Mahlon and Chilion also died! Now, widowed and childless, Naomi had no means of support. She was destitute as well as grief- stricken. Realizing there was nothing she could do except head back to her homeland, the ageing woman advised Ruth and Orpah to return to their family homes. At least that way, Naomi believed, they would be cared for, and may even find happiness in a future marriage. However, with so much heartache to deal with, Naomi barely noticed the little root of bitterness that was starting to burrow its way into her soul.

But Ruth refused to leave her mother-in-law, and instead of choosing resentment in response to her own personal heartache, she chose acceptance ... not only for what had happened in the past, but also for whatever might come in the future. In some of the most moving words in Scripture, the young Moabite widow not only declares her loyalty to her mother-in-law, but also takes an oath binding her to Yahweh, the God of Israel:

Entreat me not to leave you,
Or to turn back from following after you;
For wherever you go, I will go;
And wherever you lodge, I will lodge;

Your people shall be my people,
And your God, my God.
Where you die, I will die,
And there will I be buried.
The LORD do so to me, and more also,
If anything but death parts you and me.

RUTH 1:16–17

And so the two widowed women headed off on the long and difficult journey from Moab to Bethlehem in Judah. Naomi was going home, to a place and people she knew well and to a situation where she knew that God had made provision for the widow. She would not starve, and would most likely be welcomed back, but Naomi didn't allow hope to blossom. Her loss was great, and in those long days and nights of trailing along with other travellers for safety, she started to blame God for all of her woes. And the root pushed down a little deeper into her heart each day.

Ruth, on the other hand, was leaving behind all that she knew and loved. Her husband was gone, and she had made a decision to say farewell to the rest of her family and head for a foreign land, with a foreign God, and to live with people who might not even accept her. For Ruth, the future looked anything but easy. But her attitude of acceptance, accompanied by her new declaration of faith, left no room for the weeds of bitterness to grow in her young heart. She was at peace.

By the time the long and tedious journey was over, the dastardly weed was doing its worst in Naomi's heart. There was no joyful response to those who came to welcome her home. Instead, a miserable Naomi announced that she didn't want them to call her by her given name (Naomi means "pleasant"), as life had not been pleasant to her.

"Call me Mara, for the Almighty has dealt very bitterly with me. I went out full, and the LORD has brought me home again empty ... the Almighty has afflicted me" (Ruth 1:20–21).

Our memory often plays tricks on us when we are burdened with other things. When she had left Bethlehem with her family, life was, in fact, very different to how she now remembered it – otherwise they wouldn't have left! And there is no suggestion that what had happened to her was in any way a punishment from God, yet that is how she described it. In mercy, God was using these tragic events to bring Naomi back to blessing, and to enable Ruth to be introduced into Israel's story. His plan was much greater than Naomi could, or wanted, to see as she wearily trudged her way back to Bethlehem. The weed of bitterness was depriving her of the ability to rest in the purposes and provision of God.

Thankfully, it was not so with Ruth. In spite of the continuing difficult circumstances and a grief-stricken mother-in-law, she did her best to keep them both alive, working hard in the fields day after day. In the process Ruth discovered that Yahweh "is able to do exceedingly abundantly above all that we ask or think", long before the apostle Paul wrote those words in Ephesians 3:20.

Ruth's love and faithfulness softened the older woman's heart until she was able to see beyond herself once again. In Naomi's life the weeding began, leaving room once more for wise thinking and excited anticipation. Life was not the disaster she had thought; neither was God merely sticking the pieces of their lives together again – He was giving them something completely new. It was time for Naomi to rid herself of anger and resentment; to act on what she knew, and trust in the God who had not left her without a redeemer.

Then later, when Naomi held her little grandson, Obed, in her arms for the first time, she knew that what the women of Bethlehem said was true:

"And may he [Obed] be to you a restorer of life and a nourisher of your old age; for your daughter-in-law, who loves you, who is better to you than seven sons, has borne him" (Ruth 4:15).

Yet none of them knew that from Obed's line would come the Messiah!

The heartache that visited Naomi and Ruth was undoubtedly affected by how each of the women reacted to it. "Pain is inevitable," author Barbara Johnson says, "but misery is optional!" "We decide how we will react to the pain that inevitably comes to us all," she continues in her book *Stick a Geranium in Your Hat and Be Happy*.[1]

How true. We choose denial or acceptance. We choose anger or forgiveness. We choose bitterness or loving trust. The choice is ours to make. The outcome has significant consequences for our present peace and future healing.

When heartache hits, we need to remember that misery is an optional extra – we can choose not to accept it.

Planting – what is good

"Leave him alone, you big bully!"

My knuckles rattled against the window-pane in an effort to frighten off the old crow. He was stealing the food we had left out for the smaller feathered visitors to our garden, and disturbing my early morning observations in the process. Hunching my shoulders upwards against the cool nip in the air, I heard the toaster pop. Mornings are not meant for speed, so I lingered a little longer, hugging a mug of hot tea.

The warm steam tickled my nose as I sipped the brew. Winter was definitely on its way. The telltale signs of frost glistening on the car roof drew my eyes outside once more. I wondered if the year-old can of de-icer would still manage to spray. That's when I noticed my favourite camellia, standing like a frozen statue at the corner of the garage. Surveying the pathetic-looking stiff shrub, a sickening sadness rose to meet the tea I was attempting to swallow. Suddenly, a rather silly little prayer came from my lips. Hearing the words bounce back took me by surprise. I suppose it's because I had never prayed for a plant before – or since! But this was important to me.

"Lord, please don't let this plant die! Not this one – please?"

The focus of my prayer was not just any pretty flowering shrub that could easily be replaced by a visit to the nearest garden centre. This camellia was altogether special. It had brought the first hint of joy to my heart when I purchased it at the butterfly farm a mere two weeks after our younger daughter, Joy, had died. I couldn't bring home a butterfly from that amazing place, so I brought home the next best thing: a small cutting that would one day flower and attract butterflies to my own garden. At least, that was the plan.

The butter settled in little puddles on my toast as I recalled that most difficult of nights. Before the dawn had a chance to colour the sky, God had used a silk butterfly to illustrate what was happening to our brave little one as she lay dying. Watching the light shining through the pretty fabric insect attached to her bedside lamp had had a profound effect on my soul.

"Catherine," God whispered, ever so gently, as I carried our daughter to the gates of Heaven. *"Look at the butterfly – that's what is happening to Joy at this very minute. She's changing, Catherine – I am changing her – completely!"*

In the few minutes it took for Joy to make the journey from Earth to Heaven, the truth dawned on me. She had had to struggle so much in her short thirteen years; her frail little body totally ineffective to meet the challenges of anything that resembled a normal childhood. But not for much longer – soon she would be free! The promise observed in a silk butterfly illustrated precisely the words spoken by our Saviour Himself in Revelation 21:4–5:

"And God will wipe away every tear from their eyes; there shall be no more death, nor sorrow, nor crying. There shall be no more pain, for the former things have passed away ... Behold, I make all things new."

As a hot tear dropped from my cheek to hers, I received unexpected courage to say the words I felt our little girl needed to hear.

"Don't be afraid, sweetheart ... it's OK to go. Soon you are going to fly, like the butterfly – only, straight to Heaven!"

And soar she did.

Then one year later, exactly to the day, my little stick of a camellia plant gave me two of the most beautiful pink blooms I have ever seen. With two daughters in Heaven, we now had two blooms on earth!

Reluctantly dragging myself back from my memories, I was certain of one thing – I didn't want this plant to die! This particular horticultural emergency called for an expert gardener, and I knew exactly who to ring.

So, for the next few weeks I carefully and lovingly followed my mother's instructions on reviving my frost-damaged plant. A well-sheltered place was found, protecting it from the wind and allowing it to draw heat from the house. I also paid more than the usual self-centred attention to the weather forecast. Then, when frost was expected, I wrapped my precious memory-maker in gardener's fleece. Never was a plant more mollycoddled – well, in our house, at least!

There was one other piece of advice that undoubtedly helped with the survival of my camellia. Something that, had it not been for the frost incident, I would never have found out. Camellias need to grow in special soil – ericaceous soil, to be precise. So if the frost hadn't killed it, then the wrong type of soil eventually would have. When I had replanted my precious plant after our recent house move, I had inadvertently used the wrong soil.

I told you this gardening was hard work!

And the same goes for our souls. It takes time and energy to cultivate what is good in our hearts. What grows there, and the subsequent quality of growth, depends on what is planted in the first place.

Like me, you probably know people who never seem to exhibit any resentment or anger over the difficulties that come into their lives. They display the calm, peaceful exterior of a swan on water, without all the energetic paddling that goes on beneath the surface. Complete trust in God is as natural to them as breathing, whilst questioning Him is as alien as darkness in an Arctic summer. Weeds will blow in their direction, but without the right type of soil, there is nowhere for them to take root. And usually, those of us who look on are astonished at what we see, longing that we could be more like them.

How can this be?

Given the same circumstances, what is it that keeps some people so emotionally together when the rest of us would fall apart?

Undoubtedly, the soil in their soul – the godly attitude they display – is not something they have managed to conjure up all by themselves. Positive thinking alone is not enough. However, the prophet Isaiah gives us some insight into their secret: "You will keep him in perfect peace, Whose mind is stayed on You, Because he trusts in You" (Isaiah 26:3).

Peace starts in the mind, before it reaches the heart. What we think, how we think and whom we think about are the first lessons in the planting that we need to engage in. The root of bitterness can quickly take hold because of wrong thoughts, fertilized by resentment and anger, towards others or towards God. Therefore if we are going to experience God's perfect peace, the first thing we need to do is to keep our minds focused on Jesus. The more we concentrate on Him, the easier it will be to trust Him – and that will result in God's peace. It's what we might call the "cycle of faith". Correct thinking leads to wise action, which results in inner peace.

Negativity, on the other hand, is a weed magnet. It can never allow goodness to flourish. Instead it will invariably cause damage and destruction. How much better it is for us to develop spiritual positive thinking that concentrates on Christ, and the power available to us through His Holy Spirit.

That was what Paul was recommending to the church at Philippi. Whatever else was going on in their lives, he wanted them to meditate on what was important and beneficial to them. That, in turn, would help them deal with all the distressing stuff that was filling their day:

Finally, brethren, whatever things are true, whatever things are noble, whatever things are just, whatever things are pure, whatever things are lovely, whatever things are of good report, if there is any virtue and if there is anything praiseworthy – meditate on these things.

PHILIPPIANS 4:8

The apostle wanted to make sure that Satan, the father of lies, would not be allowed to damage the souls of these young converts by what he was enticing them to think.

Even today it is so easy to fall into the trap of negative thinking. We think that no one cares; that God has sent heartache to punish us; that we are unlovely and unloved; that our pain can only bring disaster. Subsequently, as we feed on these negative and untrue thoughts, they initiate a response of anger and resentment. Weeds spring up, leaving no room for what is good and helpful to germinate.

Conversely, Paul is encouraging us to engage in positive, wholesome thinking – starting with truth. What better way is there to stand against Satan's lies than to meditate on the things that are true? Elsewhere Paul reinforces this teaching by describing truth as the belt in God's armour that holds everything together (Ephesians 6:14). Before Paul ever brought the gospel to Philippi, Jesus had described Himself in John 14:6 as "*the* Truth" (my italics) – the One who holds us together, if we trust in Him. This, in turn, powerfully reinforces the words spoken by Jesus in John 8:32, 36: "And you shall know the truth, and the truth shall make you free ... Therefore if the Son makes you free, you shall be free indeed."

All too often, we blame circumstances for all of our misery, and undoubtedly much damage is caused by personal heartache. But sometimes we are slow to recognize the prison we condemn ourselves to, by allowing a wrong attitude to become the soil we plant in.

During the writing of this book I have come through an excessively busy and stressful year. The circumstances of family life, church and ministry have weighed heavily – and, reluctant though I am to admit it, they have turned me into a grump at times! There have been occasions when I have been trying to plant in the wrong kind of soil: the soil of bad attitude.

Add self-absorbed thinking to the mix, and discouragement soon sets in – perfect conditions for the devil's lies to take root and grow. Thankfully, the One who has declared Himself as "the Truth" dwells in us. It is so liberating to meditate on "whatever things are true" – and that always starts with directing our thoughts towards Jesus. Often simply whispering His name starts the comforting process of turning the barren soil. Once we consciously think of who He is, and the magnitude of what that means to us, and for us, we can feel the weeds of sorrow and self-pity loosen deep within.

Praise is a great hoe!

Personally, I have found that there is nothing quite like time spent with the door shut. Singing songs centred on the Saviour, or reading God's Word out loud, will soon fill our minds with what is good. The result is the planting of seedlings of trust and acceptance, which then bloom into flowers of peace and usefulness. Allowing what we already know about God and His plan for our lives to come to the fore once more will expel what we don't know, or aren't sure of.

Before long we will discover that the godly attitude encouraged by Philippians 4:8 will soon translate into the fearless declaration of Philippians 4:13: "I can do all things through Christ who strengthens me."

For some of us that will mean the strength to accomplish many things, which, given the circumstances, would normally be impossible: facing the future alone; standing up to an unfair boss; going through major surgery; attending the funeral of a dear one; rebuilding a failed business; restoring a broken relationship; enduring a difficult marriage or forgiving someone who has caused deep hurt.

As we make the choice to ditch negativity and fix our eyes instead on Jesus, trusting in Him, we will find that God keeps His side of the bargain. Perfect peace will be ours to enjoy (Isaiah 26:3).

Developing a godly attitude will undoubtedly help us to care for our souls. Other necessary work is harder to get your head around, especially when it involves planting gratitude. Just where, and how, does thankfulness enter the equation when your life has been deeply traumatized?

It is easy to identify with Paul's advice to Timothy when he instructs the young man to "endure hardship as a good soldier" (2 Timothy 2:3). The verb "endure" smacks of surviving something tough; of making it through to the very end. It conjures up in our minds that picture of grinning and bearing it; of stoically sticking something out to its conclusion. We understand the analogy. We can even feel a bit of a martyr complex developing, especially when we take the words out of context. And that's how they are often used – out of context. For the tough amongst us, the misuse of these words restricts us to a persistent "pulling your socks up" lifestyle – struggling to deal with situations that we do not need to face alone.

Somehow, we favour handling hardship by ourselves rather

than admitting that we need help. The self-sufficiency that is produced when we "endure", in the wrong sense of the word, is a dangerous little seedling to plant. It has the habit of producing the weeds of negativity and self-pity – a "woe is me" scenario in our souls.

However, if we had to choose between the advice proffered in 1 Thessalonians 5:18 and 2 Timothy 2:3, I would dare to guess that we would initially choose the latter. 1 Thessalonians 5:18 introduces us to the concept of developing a thankful heart – whatever our circumstances: "in everything give thanks; for this is the will of God in Christ Jesus for you."

"Giving thanks" isn't a huge problem. It's the "in everything" bit that can prove difficult.

How can we display gratitude when we have been bereaved; abused; betrayed; diseased; abandoned; violated – and a host of other despicable adjectives? What is going on here? Is God expecting a step too far from us? Does He really expect us to be glad that misfortune or disaster has blasted its way through our lives?

Well, no, that's not what is actually being suggested.

For example, we are neither asked nor expected to be thankful for all that has happened to us because of the results of the fall. God would not look for our gratitude for situations that have developed because of original sin. He is holy and takes no pleasure from sin, or its consequences. As we have already seen, we do not live as God had originally intended us to. Neither does He play some kind of cosmic "look-at-how-they-handle-suffering" game. In fact, in Lamentations 3:33 God explains that He does not willingly afflict the children of men. And Hebrews 4:15 describes Jesus as One who sympathizes with our weaknesses.

Instead, God is asking us, in this difficult verse in 1 Thessalonians, to be thankful "*in* everything". Running alongside all we are going through is God's perfect plan for us, as well as His bigger picture for mankind. He wants us to be thankful for that. We are multi-layered individuals. Each layer is a vital component in what God wants us to become. Pain and loss are layers we would rather do without, but that is not possible in this scene of time. So God ensures that these unwanted layers are even more precious than gold after the firing process is over, producing something beautiful for now and eternity (1 Peter 1:6–7). What happens is that God takes what is broken and painful, and makes it useful again. He wastes nothing in our lives, showing us that our pain is important to Him. That is also something for which to be thankful.

The wonderful medical missionary, Dr Helen Roseveare, lived through the Congo rebellion of the 1960s. Helen dedicated her life and skills to the people of that very needy African country. She not only worked in jungle hospitals – she built them! Lives were saved; children were fed; schools rose where education had been previously unobtainable. She loved these people and worked tirelessly to bring them the message of Jesus, as well as improvements to their health.

Then disaster struck. Rebel forces invaded missionary compounds. Hospitals were burnt; schools demolished. Villagers went into hiding in the deep jungle territory. Foreign missionaries were imprisoned in dreadful conditions. A number of them were executed by illegal firing squads.

Helen herself twice stood in line awaiting the same fate – but each time was spared at the last minute. During that time of incarceration the godly missionary doctor was beaten, brutalized and raped. Helen has testified often of her ordeal and isn't afraid to speak honestly about the appalling issues she had to face. The message of 1 Thessalonians 5:18 is one she addresses frequently.

"How can I thank you for this?" she asked the Lord, after having her teeth kicked out by a rebel boot.

Movingly, she explains how God replied to her question with one of His own.

"Can you thank Me, Helen, for trusting you with this experience, even if I never tell you why?"

The hundreds of thousands of people who have heard her story would say, like me, that they could tell her some of the reason "why" – because, through her public testimony, we have been drawn closer to the Jesus she loves and has served so faithfully. God has taken that horrendous experience and turned it around for His glory, and for our benefit.

Helen didn't allow resentment and bitterness to take root in her soul. Instead she planted thankfulness – not for what happened, but for what was running alongside it. She saw God's bigger plan for her life, for our lives, and for the people she loved in the Congo.

That's why she was able to be thankful.

Cultivating prayer – the upward look

The ward had settled into night mode.

Tilted Anglepoise lamps reflected dim light against cream walls, displaying the need for a more colourful paint job. The excitement of the evening had passed, after a local television celebrity had called into the ward to visit his young nephew. Other visitors hadn't the wit to leave him alone when he had rushed to the hospital after his slot in the news programme had ended. To me, giving autographs seemed so trivial when compared with his nephew's diagnosis of leukaemia. Unfortunately, he didn't seem to know when to leave his celebrity status behind either. Shaking my hand, the man introduced himself, adding, "You may have seen me on television."

I was underwhelmed. He was embarrassed.

A high-profile job paled into insignificance in a small ward housing four very sick children, one of whom was his nephew. Another was our elder daughter. Sickness takes no account of status – celebrity or otherwise.

Now that the fuss had died down, quietness reigned, the silence barely interrupted by the bleeping of monitors and the hiss of oxygen bubbling through humidifiers. All four little persons were fast asleep – or at least, not awake.

For those of us left behind, after the other visitors have headed home, night-time in hospital becomes thinking time. Consultants have come and gone; physiotherapists have done their worst (or, should I say, best!); X-rays, tests and procedures have all been completed for another day. Only what is essential will now be allowed to disturb the healing benefits of sleep.

Consequently, mummies and daddies are left with time to think. Often it's more than they really want, as time seems to stretch on forever in a darkened ward.

I reached forward to stroke Cheryl's hand. Its small size belied her ten years; her skin, as soft as silk, was almost transparent. She had beautiful hands. Hands that would have looked just right practising scales or stretched in ballet pose – if things had been different.

"You need your nails cut, Cheryl," I whispered. "I must get Granny to bring her nail scissors with her tomorrow."

She didn't flinch at my caressing touch, hadn't done so for four days now – not as much as a blink. And I missed her already.

"What will I do when you're gone, sweetheart?"

Stray tears soaked into the quilt, as my fingers ran through her wavy, blonde hair. It was barely eighteen days to Christmas, and standing at the foot of her cot, the doctor had said those words again today:

"She's very sick."

She wasn't telling me anything I didn't already know. "I don't think she'll see Christmas," she added, as if I hadn't understood what she was trying to tell me the first time.

"She's said that before, hasn't she, pet? And she was wrong then!"

Trying to compose myself, I blew my nose as quietly as I could into the handkerchief I'd retrieved from my pocket. I didn't want the little boy's granny to see me upset. She was resting quietly beside him, and had enough worries of her own.

"All of your little friends' mummies are meeting for a party tonight, Cheryl," I said, hoping that the change of subject would lift my ever-darkening mood. And for a short time I occupied myself with thoughts of the Christmas fellowship night, which would now be in full swing. I smiled, wondering who would be the one to announce the expected arrival of another baby into our group. I could hardly remember the last time we hadn't had such an announcement during our quarterly get-togethers. Our Bible study girls were a fertile lot!

But the diversionary tactics didn't last. Perhaps the doctor would be right this time. I had never known Cheryl to remain unconscious for so long. The intravenous antibiotics were making very little impact on the virulent pneumonia. The physiotherapist's efforts appeared ineffective on her infection-clogged lungs. I didn't know what to do. I wasn't ready to lose her yet.

"Hello, dear – how's things?"

The greeting interrupted my thoughts, as I quickly turned towards the voice I recognized.

"What are you doing here? The party can't be over already!"

"Oh, they don't need me," the late visitor said, holding me in a caring embrace. "It was fun, but I couldn't get you out of my mind. So I slipped away – and everyone sends you their love, with kisses for Cheryl!"

Bending over her little sleeping head, she tenderly delivered the kisses sent by all of the precious friends God had sent to walk this long journey with me and my family. As I rested back in the chair to hear all the news, my friend took over the job of stroking Cheryl. We laughed together as quietly as we could about all that had happened before she had left the party. I caught up with whose children were doing what, and what Christmas plans were being made by my friends. But I had an inkling that this was not why this dear friend had called so late at night, especially as she had three children of her own tucked up at home.

"And how about you?" she asked tenderly.

"Well, the doctors don't see much change in Cheryl, I'm afraid. There's not much good news."

"I didn't ask about Cheryl," she replied, gently patting the motionless form beside her. "I want to know how you are."

"Tired."

She waited; her silence not uncomfortable, but a loving expression of kind understanding.

"And I don't know what to pray for."

She nodded, encouraging me to open my heart.

"Cheryl is so sick – I don't want her to suffer any more. But I don't want to lose her, so – I don't know what to pray for. And I'm so tired!"

We sat without words for a while, my friend's hands now cupping mine.

"And anyway," I gushed, "God doesn't seem to be listening to my prayers at the minute."

There, it was out!

I was feeling incapable of using the very gift that God so graciously offers to all of His children – prayer. That ability to converse with the One who knows us better than anyone else was blocked by the emotional exhaustion that is the companion of heartache. My mind was over-thinking everything. If I prayed for Cheryl to be free from suffering, then God might take her away. In spite of preparing the family for Cheryl's death, now that it seemed close, I didn't want to face it. If I prayed for God to heal her, I knew it would only be for a little while, and soon we would be right back here again. That didn't seem fair either. And, anyway, I had recently convinced myself into thinking that God didn't answer *my* prayers – so what was the point of praying?

My eyes were so focused on the physical battle for our child's life that they had been averted from Jesus. Thankfully, in matters of the human heart, He understands. And that night He sent a human voice to tell me so.

"Why don't you give her to me for a little while?"

The quiet words cut through the air, puzzling me for a split second.

"Why don't you let *me* pray for Cheryl?" my friend continued, as if what she was saying was simple common sense. "I can take her to the Lord until you are rested. Let me carry this burden for you – I will pray continually for God's will for her life, until you are ready to take it up again."

Looking into those thoughtful eyes, I could almost hear the prophet Elijah's words to the widow of Zarephath centuries earlier.

"Give me your son," he had said firmly after the boy's sudden death. When the distraught mother placed her boy in his willing arms, Elijah carried him into God's presence through prayer. He cried out to the Lord, "O LORD my God, I pray, let this child's soul come back to him" (1 Kings 17:19, 21). In that instance God's answer was a miracle – the boy was raised to life!

Elijah was willing to do for that grief-stricken mother what she couldn't do for herself – take her son to God.

In my weariness of soul I wasn't even looking for a miracle. I simply considered this request an offer of spiritual love – one mother to another. And it instantly brought relief and comfort to my soul. I wouldn't have to try to work out what I should be praying for. I could spend these days loving Cheryl, while someone else did the interceding. And I trusted this ministering angel – a woman of God, who knew how to pray.

"Thank you – I'd like that," were the only words I could muster.

It was all change when I returned from saying goodbye to my

friend at the door of the ward. Cheryl had been turned over, her little cheek pink from lying motionless on the pillow. And as I took her hand in mine, I prayed. I never stopped praying for her; I just didn't have to use words like "die" or "heal" or anything else difficult or conflicting. I simply thanked God for sending Cheryl into our lives, knowing that somewhere on the motorway another was storming the gates of Heaven on her behalf. And my heart was at peace.

My friend only had to carry Cheryl in prayer for another two days, until Jesus crept into the ward to lift her into His strong arms and take her home. Cheryl died just two weeks before Christmas, when she was only ten years old.

Why is it that some of us find prayer difficult? Why do we make this amazing privilege of conversing with the God who made us so complicated? Could it be that we are afraid that God isn't going to give us the answer we want? Or is it that we doubt that God knows what is best for us? Often I have found that it can be as simple as not knowing how to pray. Those closest to Jesus, the disciples, had that problem too, and so they asked Him to teach them how to pray. In response, Jesus taught them the simplest of prayers, as recorded in Matthew 6:5–13.

We have a tendency to over-complicate prayer, instead of using it as a mode of communicating with the One who loves us more than any other. Prayer does not require fancy words, or structured grammar. There is no right or wrong way; no minimum or maximum time allocation; no suitable or unsuitable place to pray; and nothing about which you cannot speak with God.

In prayer we can seek God's forgiveness; worship; request; intercede for others and with others; be encouraged, enlightened, informed; and listen – to what He wants to say to us. Prayer should be our highest priority and first port of call, whether our life's day is sunny or stormy. As we develop this special relationship with our Heavenly Father, we will become more and more aware of all that is available to us through Him. Then we won't find it so hard. Instead of appearing like work, we will find it a delight. Instead of watching the clock, we will find ourselves praying "without ceasing" (1 Thessalonians 5:17), discussing our every situation with the Lord.

Much of my earlier problem with prayer was because I had a tendency to pray answers, rather than requests. I often told God what I wanted, and how I felt was the best way for a situation to be resolved. Was it any wonder that I was disappointed when I didn't get the answer I was expecting? Often our perception of unanswered prayer is distorted by the limitations we have set on God. We label prayer as "unanswered" if God doesn't give us what we want!

Yet throughout Scripture God constantly encourages us to come to Him, especially with the hard things. He is forever inviting us to make Him our burden-bearer. His longing is for our good; His willingness to provide us with all of our needs knows no bounds.

"Call to Me," the Lord says, "and I will answer you, and show you great and mighty things, which you do not know" (Jeremiah 33:3).

"Cast your burden on the LORD, and He shall sustain you," the Psalmist encourages us (Psalm 55:22).

"Ask, and it will be given to you", Jesus tells His disciples (Luke 11:9).

Each of these verses contains wonderful and precious promises, yet sometimes when we "call" or "cast" or "ask", the answer doesn't come as quickly as we want, or feel that we need. And sitting in God's waiting-room can be one of the hardest things we do.

However, prayer is not a quick fix; neither does it deliver God on a string. Our Heavenly Father is not there for our use or misuse. Prayer is about God's desire towards us, and our developing relationship with Him. God knows our frame; He especially knows all about our impatience. That's why Jesus said, "that men always ought to pray and not lose heart" (Luke 18:1). He also knows when we have reached an end of ourselves and don't know how to pray any more. What a comfort that is!

"Likewise the Spirit also helps in our weaknesses. For we do not know what we should pray for as we ought, but the Spirit Himself makes intercession for us with groanings which cannot be uttered" (Romans 8:26).

Imagine – when we can't find the right words, the Spirit speaks on our behalf! God does not want to leave us floundering. He is for us ... each and every step of the way.

That's why we need to constantly cultivate prayer in our lives. It takes care and attention – but it's worth it. Often it will be instantly rewarding, filling our minds and hearts with peace as our knowledge of God increases. At other times it requires patience. God's answer may not always be immediately obvious, but it is promised. Patience, however, has a reward all of its own:

Those who wait on the Lord Shall renew their strength;
They shall mount up with wings like eagles,
They shall run and not be weary,
They shall walk and not faint.

ISAIAH 40:31

Teach me to wait, Lord!

Forgiving – a journey worth making

This was the day they had prayed for. The day they had waited such a long time for. How they wished it could all be over in just one day, yet deep in their hearts they knew that would be impossible. The man who could end it swiftly was a master of control; a man who obtained pleasure from the pain he inflicted on others. He would never change his "not guilty" plea, not while he still held the ace card of absolute knowledge of his crimes.

Yet as Andy Cardy, and his lovely wife Pat, sat waiting to see the man accused of their daughter's murder for the first time, they knew something he did not. God was the One who was in control – not Robert Black. It was God who had brought them safely through the past heart-breaking thirty years. Not only would they survive whatever this trial would throw at them, they were convinced that the evil man they were about to confront could do them no harm. This was one control game that Robert Black had already lost.

Andy gently touched Pat's hand as the door finally opened and a scruffy, balding man emerged. The accused looked pathetic, shackled in handcuffs as he was led in, looking more like a dog than a man. As he sat in a toughened, transparent, plastic box, Robert Black's face showed no emotion. Andy wasn't surprised at the feelings of pity that he had for this man, for God had had a long time to continue His work of grace in his own heart to get him to this day.

Now looking into the face of evil – the last face on earth his darling little girl had seen – Andy thanked God that today had come, and that he didn't hate this monster. The police had described Robert Black as one of the most dangerous men in British criminal history, but to Andy he looked like a wretched old man. Sin does that to people.

Although Andy was not looking forward to the trauma that the trial would undoubtedly bring, he knew that he and Pat were meant to be there. As the pre-trial proceedings began Andy could hear God's Word wash over him from earlier that morning – words that had brought him peace:

"Now when they bring you to the ... magistrates ... do not worry about how or what you should answer, or what you should say. For the Holy Spirit will teach you in that very hour what you ought to say" (Luke 12:11–12).

He had not been present for the earlier arraignment, when Robert Black entered his "not guilty" plea. Neither did he want to become media fodder by attending the trial, unless God wanted him to be there as His witness to what could be done with broken lives. Andy and Pat didn't want the trial to be about them – this was about justice for Jennifer. Therefore Andy did what he does about everything – he prayed. God would show him whether or not he should be at the trial.

Amazingly, when Andy showed Pat the direction and promise God had given him that morning in his daily Bible reading, she also had her Bible in her hands, opened at that very same promise! A promise that was to prove vital, getting them through the difficult days and weeks ahead. It was confirmation that God's own presence would bring them peace, as they relived every parent's worst nightmare in a very public way.

At this stage there was no jury; legal arguments took place for three days to determine which evidence would be admissible in court. Each time they made their way to the Crown Court in Belfast, Robert Black was kept at a distance in his secure box. No chance for revenge in this place! Security was tight. Yet for that devoted father, there were no thoughts of malicious intent towards the child-killer he now had to look at every day.

It had not always been so.

As a much younger man, Andy, without God in his life, was bent on finding the man who had killed his child. He had even gone as far as stalking a paedophile who had foolishly, though wrongly, confessed to killing Jennifer. After spending time in prison, the man was released, innocent of that crime – but Andy was distraught with grief and sought to do him harm. One dark night, with a large knife in his pocket, Andy cornered the man, only to run away when he saw how absolutely feeble and lily-livered he was. God had kept Andy from making a terrible mistake that night.

Yet, now, facing the true perpetrator, Andy had no feelings of hatred or vengeance towards him – even though, during those early days, Andy and Pat were privy to evidence that not even members of the jury would get to hear. He hated what Robert Black had done, and what he would continue to do if released, but he couldn't find any hatred in his heart towards him personally. At times that even surprised Andy himself. He even questioned himself on whether he had any feelings as a father. How could he not hate this monster?

But, in truth, what had happened in Andy's heart was all of God. With the passing of the years, he had not only grown older and wiser, he had grown more godly too. He was keenly aware that one day Robert Black would stand before the ultimate Judge

– the Maker of Heaven and Earth. If he had not repented before that fearful day, then Andy knew only too well the dreadful fate that would await him. Even that brought no pleasure to Andy's heart.

Now, as he looked at the former van driver turned child-killer, he felt a sadness rising in his heart for him. Did he not realize that "It is a fearful thing to fall into the hands of the living God" (Hebrews 10:31)? The vengeance of God could not be compared to the very worst that he might, at one time, have dreamt up for the murderer of his child. Hatred was too costly. Robert Black had stolen the life of his darling daughter, and destroyed the lives of many others; Andy had decided that he wouldn't let this man destroy his life as well. Yes, hatred was much too costly.

Before the jury was chosen and the trial opened to the press, Pat and Andy had to endure listening to the most horrific evidence. All the minute details of Jennifer's abduction and death were laid out before them, while Robert Black sat looking disinterested in the dock. Things that they had allowed to stay locked in the hidden recesses of their minds for thirty years were once again released. Intimate details of the horrific and bestial brutality their beautiful little girl had been subjected to before her abused body was dumped into the dam, ten miles from their home on that August afternoon, were laid bare.

These devoted, loving parents were heartbroken beyond belief during those three days. By the time they attended the church prayer meeting on the Wednesday night, Andy's tears were unremitting. Yet it was the love and support of those brothers and sisters in Christ that gave him the strength to continue to fix his eyes on Jesus.

The walk into the past had just begun.

But neither Pat nor Andy was making that dreadful journey alone. God would be right there beside them – He had promised.

The trial proper was relocated to the more intimate setting of Armagh Courthouse. Sunlight shone through the tall arched windows, the ornamental columns and finely carved woodwork displaying a prettiness that seemed out of place in a room that would soon resound with stories of horror. Little distance now separated Andy from Robert Black – he could have reached out and touched him. Yes, he could have shot him, if he had had a mind to, with no security in sight.

But Andy's thoughts were of a different kind – even with all he knew, and was about to find out, about Robert Black.

For now, it was his wife Pat who was concentrating Andy's attention and prayers. She had been put into the witness box on that first day in Armagh to tell the jury, in her own words, what happened on that fateful day – 12 August 1981.

Andy was so proud of her – the wife of his youth – the one he'd fallen in love with as a schoolboy. Pat was the first of them to find Jesus as Saviour; she was the loving, devoted mother of his five children; the one who was the strong constant in his life until he eventually trusted in Christ, a full twelve years after Jennifer's death. She had stuck with him through thick and thin – the bravest woman he had ever known – now showing that bravery to the world.

He listened as Pat explained how their nine-year-old daughter, Jennifer, had asked to cycle the short distance to see her friend that sunny afternoon. School holidays were still in full swing, and Jennifer was really making the most of the good days on her new bicycle. Andy smiled as thoughts of taking Jennifer to choose that new, red bike quickly flashed into his mind. *She loved that bike!*

Pat continued. Jennifer wasn't home when she said she'd be, and that was unusual – she was normally a very obedient child.

As Andy looked at the jury, he could sense their concern and sympathy. Even the judge appeared sombre, as the overhanging canopy above his chair cast its shadow. Meanwhile, the man in the dock, sitting with his back to Andy, slouched in his seat, unconcerned – able, yet unwilling, to fill in the blanks of the story he knew only too well.

By now Pat was speaking about Andy; how he'd come home from work with a flat tyre, and had told her not to worry. Jennifer had probably lost track of time. She was having fun with her friends. Andy felt uncomfortable in his seat; the memory of that short delay pained him even yet. Bravely Pat continued to answer questions, filling in the details of what had happened on that most dreadful of days, to the listening court. She looked tired and sad – so sad.

A phone call had revealed that Jennifer had never arrived at her friend's house. Andy and some neighbours then drove around the surrounding country lanes for a little while before calling in the police.

Then the unimaginable happened. Just before midnight, Jennifer's new red bike was found in a field, barely a mile from her home – it had been thrown over a hedge! But there was no trace of the little girl.

"Jennifer!"

Andy could hear her name echoing in the courtroom as it did on a summer evening thirty years earlier. Back then, her lovely name brought together a community in trouble-torn Northern Ireland. Neighbour had walked beside neighbour with one goal in mind – to find little Jennifer Cardy. Politics and creed melted like ice under the summer sun, as day after day, for six long days, hundreds of people searched for the missing little girl wearing a white T-shirt with strawberries on the front.

Pat snuggled up close to Andy as the prosecution barrister continued without her.

Could it really be them this eminent man was speaking about?

All the things they had hidden deep in their memories were being dragged out before these strangers. The very worst of information they had refused permission to surface, in order that they could continue to live and bring up their remaining family, was no longer owned by just a few. Everyone and his wife now knew what had happened to Jennifer in her last hours. Even pictures of her lifeless body, floating face down amongst the reeds of Maxwell's dam, were shown to these strangers.

Yes, Jennifer was dead – murdered by a monster! Her life stolen from her, and from them, by a man who had dared to admit to getting his "kicks" from sexually molesting young girls.

It was eight days into the trial before the prosecution was allowed to reveal Robert Black's previous crimes. In great detail the twelve unfortunate members of the jury had to listen to descriptions of what the man in the dock had already been found guilty of. Many of them fought back tears, as they had no option but to listen to the catalogue of atrocities listed by counsel.

Susan Maxwell, age eleven, murdered. Caroline Hogg, age five, murdered. Susan Harper, age ten, murdered. A fifteen-year-old girl – a failed abduction. A six-year-old girl abducted, sexually assaulted, a bag put over her head; she was shoved head first into a sleeping bag and thrown into the back of Black's van. Mercifully, it was during this heinous crime that Black was caught in the act, and the child's life was saved.

With a courtroom in visible shock, the accused man simply fiddled with his hearing aid – a mere arm's length from the father of one of his innocent victims. But Robert Black cared no more for the Cardy family than he did for all the other families. Neither twinge of remorse, nor glimpse of regret, ever once slipped from the murderer's mask of cold indifference.

For six weeks Andy and Pat continued to sit in that courtroom; wounds made bare; sorrow revisited. When the "guilty" verdict was at last announced, the very walls of Armagh courtroom seemed to sigh with relief, its occupants weeping openly. From court clerk to juror to press – to Andy, Pat and their remaining family – the place was awash with tears. Except for one man – the man in the dock.

Then in a display of magnanimity Andy Cardy crossed the courtroom and shook hands with each of Robert Black's defence team, while his lovely wife embraced the defence barrister.

Andy and Pat Cardy know all about forgiveness. They are themselves forgiven people – forgiven by the only One who can truly forgive: the Lord Jesus Christ. This trial was not about vengeance, it was about justice – justice for a pretty, dark-haired child, whose cheeks fell into dimples every time a smile crossed her face: their beloved Jennifer.

And God is also all about justice.

He has declared that "the wages of sin is death". There is punishment to be faced by each of us for our sin, but God extends His mercy to us, as the verse continues with the wonderful words: "but the gift of God is eternal life in Christ Jesus our Lord" (Romans 6:23).

Our part is repentance. Forgiveness can only follow an honest sorrow for and a turning away from sin, and is only available though the redeeming sacrifice made for us on the cross by God's Son.

Robert Black has never repented of his sin, nor sought forgiveness from the only One who can give it. In spite of this, the child-murderer is loved by God, who hates his crimes, yet is willing to forgive Robert Black, should he repent.

This is hard theology!

Surely Robert Black doesn't deserve mercy!

Then again, it wouldn't be mercy if he did!

Neither does Robert Black deserve anything other than hatred from Andy Cardy. In the eyes of the world, Andy would be justified if he were twisted by bitterness towards the killer of his child, or if anger rose in his heart with every thought of that man.

Yet, nothing could be further from the truth. You see, forgiveness is about more than the utterance of a few words. For many people that is where it will start, but the truly important thing is what we do with all the feelings that arise from the injury which has been inflicted on us. An unforgiving spirit results in hatred, bitterness and anger: destructive weeds that perpetuate the assault on our souls.

Over the many years it has taken to bring Robert Black to justice, Andy has allowed God to deal with all the ungodly attitudes that could have furthered the destructive nature of the murderer's crime. There is now not one tiny shred of malice left in Andy's heart towards the man he saw in Armagh Courthouse for six long weeks. Instead, pity, sadness, and even feelings of "love for Christ's sake" have been the occupants of this godly man's heart.

As the weeks of the trial had progressed, the pain hadn't lessened, but neither did the profound words of Joseph in Genesis 50:20, which had come to mean so much to Andy's heart: "But as for you, you meant evil against me; but God meant it for good, in order to bring it about as it is this day, to save many people alive."

Robert Black may have planned and executed evil towards Jennifer, but God has been able to turn that around in Andy's life into something good.

"I'm into Kingdom building, Catherine," Andy said, as I spoke with him. "I'm raring to tell people about the Saviour! I couldn't do that if I hated Robert Black."

His face broke into a broad smile as I recognized that this man is the genuine article. His life declares what his lips have not yet said. Forgiveness for Andy is living as Christ intended him to live, unhampered by negative, destructive emotions. It has been a journey worth making, for it has already touched many lives now and for eternity.

"You may not understand it – at times, I can't understand it myself – but I have a fabulous, wonderful contentment. Only God could do that!"

I couldn't agree more.

"This was the LORD's doing; it is marvellous in our eyes" (Psalm 118:23).

Notes

1. Barbara Johnson, *Stick a Geranium in Your Hat and Be Happy!*, Word, 1990, p. 4.

Taking a closer look

- Read Hebrews 12:14–15. Carefully examine your heart, and if there is any weeding to be done, ask God to help you start the process.

- The book of Ruth contains only four short chapters. Have a look to see what happens when we refuse to allow bitterness to take root.

- Memorize Philippians 4:8–9 and absorb the words – after all, that's what Paul encourages us to do in verse 8 when he says to "meditate on these things".

- Explore the meaning of 1 Thessalonians 5:18 for yourself, and take time to list the things that you can be thankful for in your situation.

- What can we learn from Jesus' prayer life in these verses: Luke 6:12; Matthew 14:23; Mark 14:32–41; John 17:9–26?

- If you have never personally sought God's forgiveness, why not do so today? See 1 John 1:8–9.

FIVE

REAPING THE RESULTS

Don't waste your pain

"I've changed my mind!" the young woman screamed. "I don't want to have the baby now!"

"Too late for that, dear. We're almost there – just give me one big push when the next pain comes."

"No! I told you I want to stop! I can't do this!"

We all braced ourselves for another onslaught from a very distressed young mother. She was kicking, screaming, biting and a whole lot more; she was just beside herself with terror. A long labour should have already produced her firstborn, if it were not for the young woman's inability to realize that if she would just push when a contraction came, then the pain would soon be over.

"This is your fault!" she shouted at her young husband, who was sitting at her side looking stunned.

By now he was black and blue, his hands gripped so tightly by those of his wife that it was a wonder his circulation was still functioning! All his attempts at trying to calm her had not only failed, they had been abandoned some time before. His face no longer changed colour with embarrassment – it stayed a permanent shade of white.

"Next time you want a baby you can have it yourself!"

The labour suite was now filling up with staff trying to help with what was becoming an impossible situation. I was holding a leg, as was another midwife – supporting her physically and also trying to ease her exhaustion a little. From my vantage point I could see the little tufts of hair – one good push would bring this baby into the world, but her constant fighting against the pain, and us, was now obstructing the delivery.

There was more sweat in that delivery room than in a ring of Sumo wrestlers! However, it had long since ceased to be funny and was now causing concern. The mother was not the only one who was exhausted. The baby was also showing signs of tiring, as its heart rate was beginning to show little dips on the foetal monitor.

The midwife in charge of the delivery was quickly examining her options, knowing that she needed to get this baby out soon, before the situation became dangerous. There was no more time to try to reason with the patient. Just as she was about to send for the anaesthetist, the door of the room opened, and the rather stern face of the senior midwife appeared. She didn't need to enter the room to know what was going on – the noise had probably reached every corner of the maternity hospital by this stage! She was fully aware of our dilemma.

Once the commotion surrounding the current contraction had passed, the senior midwife walked straight up to the patient. Losing no time, she quickly cupped the young woman's face firmly in both of her hands. Stepping back in silence, we wondered what she was going to do. And looking straight into the young woman's terrified eyes, the senior midwife spoke to her resolutely:

"Listen to me!" she said with a stern note of concern. "Don't waste your pain. That pain is going to give you a beautiful baby. Now don't waste it – use it!"

We all stood by dumbfounded at such a profoundly compelling statement, a stunned silence now replacing the incessant noise of the previous few hours.

"Next time a pain comes – you PUSH!" was the senior midwife's final passing shot as she stepped back.

And no sooner were the words out of her mouth than the next forceful contraction came. And what did the young woman do? She pushed – with all her might!

Seconds later, the air in the room was filled with a different type of screaming – the sound of new life from one healthy baby, and the cries of delight of two proud new parents. Soon laughter was bouncing off the walls as both mum and dad celebrated the birth of their new little daughter. The pain she had fought against ended up bringing joy into their lives – once the young woman decided to use it, rather than waste it.

I have never forgotten those wise words from the senior midwife that day: "Don't waste your pain!"

In fact, I've lost count of the number of times that God has whispered those words in my ear, reminding me to use every painful experience I go through to produce whatever He wants to deliver in my life.

We are told in Ecclesiastes 3:11 that God "has made everything beautiful in its time". Those words are contained in what I call the "time chapter", where the writer explains that "To everything there is a season, A time for every purpose under heaven" (verse 1). We read of the happy and the sad, the good and the bad; of love and hate, war and peace. The extremes of living all have a season in our lives – but we are told that none of them are without purpose in God's great plan.

We are promised that all the things we see as ugly, pointless or painful can become the exact opposite – something beautiful and useful. Unfortunately, just like the labouring mother, we can delay the good that God has for us by constant struggling against what He has allowed in our lives. Sometimes it takes a firm reminder to help us realize that what we are experiencing is not the end of the story. Pain is not where everything stops. Rather, it is the vehicle through which God, with our co-operation, can bring His blessing back into our lives.

The apostle Paul was a vivid example to the many new believers, both Gentile and Jewish, of the spiritual benefits that come from suffering. He tells them in Philippians 4:11: "I have learned in whatever state I am, to be content". Then he goes on to tell them that the same God who had looked after him would be the One who would "supply all [their] need according to His riches in glory by Christ Jesus" (verse 19). Paul was saying that they shouldn't be afraid of what was happening to them at that time, or what might happen to them in the future. God would take care of them, just as He had taken care of him. Paul's suffering was not wasted; it was already impacting the lives of others.

He had been shipwrecked three times; had endured beatings; was publicly stoned; imprisoned three times; hated by many wherever he travelled, and had no place of permanent abode. Yet he said he was content!

Contentment is that feeling of satisfaction which comes from a deep acceptance both of ourselves and of our circumstances. As Christians it is the end result of a complete and absolute trust in God for who we are, and what we need now and in the future. When we reach the point of accepting our suffering as part of God's big plan for us and mankind, the burden lightens – even if the physical circumstances remain unchanged. If we add to that the truth expressed in 2 Corinthians 4:17 that "our light affliction, which is but for a moment, is working for us a far more exceeding and eternal weight of glory," then we begin to see that what we are going through also has eternal implications. It is not wasted.

I repeat, without apology: pain is not where everything stops. It is productive – when we learn to be content. God chose never to make contentment a gift. Instead, it is something we learn in the school of pain – and it is rarely an easy lesson to learn. As we work our way towards contentment we may go via the roads of anger, bitterness and even rejection of God's will. Or perhaps He will take us through the more understandable way of sorrow, misunderstanding, grief, anxiety and loss. But the lessons we are prepared to learn along the way will eventually lead us to the place of contentment that Paul spoke about.

These lessons will confirm, like no others can, that God loves us deeply; that we never need walk through our heartache alone; that God promises His presence, His peace, and the strength of Christ, through His Holy Spirit, to enable us to meet whatever each day brings. As the truth of all this shifts from our head to our heart, we learn acceptance first of all. Soon after, we will discover that contentment begins to grow – in spite of our circumstances, and in spite of our own ability. Contentment is inextricably linked with a confident belief that God knows what He is doing, even if we don't.

Acceptance and contentment should not be confused with fatalism. We do not sit idly by with a fatalistic approach to life, waiting to see what other misery will drop on our lap! Instead, God chooses to work with us, and through us, not only to fulfil His plan, but to teach us loving trust – in order that we might find contentment. The spiritual resources we need for that to happen are about more than stoically surviving the hard times.

Resources such as "love, joy, peace, patience, kindness, goodness, faithfulness, gentleness and self-control" (Galatians 5:22–23 NIV) are grown in us by the Holy Spirit. They help make us become the people God wants us to be. Yet, it may surprise us to know how some of these "fruits of the Spirit" come to be grown in our lives in the first place.

"My brethren, count it all joy when you fall into various trials," says James to those who were suffering, "knowing that the testing of your faith produces patience. But let patience have its perfect work, that you may be perfect and complete, lacking nothing" (James 1:2–4).

The pain involved in trials and testing, James says, is producing patience in us – therefore we shouldn't waste it. He goes on to say that patience develops our character, and makes us ready for anything, producing positive results from situations which would ordinarily have the opposite effect.

That's what is so amazing about God. He is able to work beyond the sin-affected laws of nature, transforming their impact into what He wants them to be, both for His glory and for our good. Our personal walk with God always adds that supernatural dimension to our lives. God turns around the damaging, negative philosophy we are bombarded with, that says: "We came from nowhere; we are here for no purpose; and when we die, that's it." In its place God's message declares that we are His special creation; each of us loved, and with purpose here on earth; finally bound for an eternity with Him when we die.

The here and now is *not* all there is.

Such powerful teaching has the ability to produce in us a sense of worth beyond anything that money or power can do. I am who I am because of Christ! My sinful past has been dealt with; my present is known to God; His plans are for my ultimate good; and my eternal future is not only secure, but "the sufferings of this present time are not worthy to be compared with the glory which shall be revealed in us" (Romans 8:18).

True contentment doesn't start with an accumulation of things; it is an attitude of heart, learnt through pain. An attitude that says I can feel deep satisfaction, whatever my situation, because of Jesus Christ.

I would never have experienced "the peace of God, which surpasses all understanding" (Philippians 4:7) if my life had not been thrown into turmoil by our daughters' shocking diagnoses of disability. It was pain that birthed a peace in my life that was at times tangible – and certainly beyond anything I can adequately explain.

I doubt that I would have sought to know God in the way that I have if my life's experience had always been trouble free. It was pain that taught me about "God my Maker, Who gives songs in the night" (Job 35:10). It was pain that sent me to His Word on more occasions than joy, enabling me to learn more about the wonderful character and plans of God.

My understanding of God's compassion would have been more limited if I hadn't cried all those tears, knowing that "You keep track of all my sorrows. You have collected all my tears in your bottle. You have recorded each one in your book" (Psalm 56:8 NLT).

At times, I wouldn't have felt His presence closer than that of any human being, if I hadn't had all my props stripped away, and learned to "Trust in the LORD with all [my] heart" (Proverbs 3:5).

When our daughters died, I was able to truly glimpse Jesus as "A Man of sorrows and acquainted with grief ", as He "[bore] our griefs And carried our sorrows" (Isaiah 53:3–4). He was the One I could trust with the horrors of such loss, believing that as I cast my burden on the Lord, He was able to sustain me (Psalm 55:22).

Pain has taken me to places with God that I had never dreamed possible, and continues to give me entrance into the lives of other hurting people.

Some of the people who have had the greatest impact on my life have been those who have personally suffered tragedy, loss or persecution. It has not been the circumstances of their heartache, or the tragic story associated with their pain that has affected me, but how they have come through. Without exception, they have been the people who have allowed God to turn their pain into gain, and have emerged without bitterness – displaying God's grace and peace.

Unfortunately there are some people who choose to fight the plan of God in their lives, and their pain is compounded because it remains pointless – without any apparent purpose. How much better if we would choose to allow God to take our broken lives and use them in ways we could never have imagined. Birthing something spiritual is not always as straightforward as physical childbirth, as often much time may pass before we begin to see results. While for others, very little of the full picture will emerge before we reach Heaven.

But, remember, God never wastes our pain. Our part is to look for the results He produces.

The gospel will prosper

My husband was accustomed to hecklers when he preached in the open air. His approach to presenting the good news of the gospel in public places was always with enthusiasm and grace. Dour, finger-wagging condemnation was not his style, so a genuine smile always accompanied his endeavours – the message is "good news", after all! However, the Bible does tell us in 1 Corinthians 1:18 that the gospel appears foolish to many people – hence the common indifference to open-air preaching, and the occasional abuse thrown at the speaker.

"It's all right for you up there to talk about God!" railed the man at the edge of the crowd.

A few of the team members tried to quieten him, but what the poor man didn't realize was that his efforts to interrupt the preaching were drawing an even larger crowd. Maybe those who stopped wanted to see what the preacher on the box would say when challenged.

"If you had my problems it would wipe that smile off your face!"

His fist was shaking and his objections were filled with sadness.

"God doesn't care about me!" he continued.

"Sir," my husband replied firmly but with kindness, "if you wait until I'm finished, then I am more than happy to speak with you privately – I believe I can show you that God does indeed care for you."

The man stood with arms crossed and face grimaced, ready for an argument with the soap-box preacher. Philip doubted that he even bothered to listen to what he had to say about a loving Saviour, who had demonstrated His love for us by dying on a Roman cross. However, as promised, my husband made a bee-line towards the man as soon as he stepped down from the little wooden box.

With his finger pointing menacingly at Philip's chest, the man repeated his earlier statements, without waiting for introductions.

"God doesn't care about me! If you knew what my life was like, you wouldn't be so quick to smile!"

"Why don't you tell me about your life?" Philip replied calmly, trying to defuse what was becoming an angry situation.

"I've got a handicapped child at home – can't do a thing for himself – and you tell me that God cares about me!"

"Oh really," my husband replied sympathetically, "I am so sorry. We have two handicapped children. I know how painful that can be."

The man stopped in his tracks – momentarily dumbfounded. Lowering his accusatory finger, he stepped back, his tone now moderated.

"You've got *two* handicapped children?"

"Yes, two daughters, who, like your son, need to have everything done for them."

Before my husband could continue, the man interjected, "How come you're smiling, then?"

For the next little while my husband stood with that man, and told him how it was Jesus who helped him to get through every day – especially the most difficult ones. Having identified with the man's pain, Philip was then able to speak to him about a Saviour who loved him, and cared for him deeply – a Saviour who could put sense back into the senselessness of his family circumstances, if he would only let Him. The sad father walked away more quietly than he had arrived. Though still not convinced that God really cared about him, he had met a man with double his problems – who, because of the grace of God, could still smile.

And later that day, as Philip cuddled his precious girls, he told them that, because of them, he was able to talk to a man about Jesus. That's reaping results!

There have been numerous occasions when God has used the key of pain to open the door of opportunity for us to share the gospel. I don't remember the last time I spoke at a meeting or event where no one shared a painful circumstance with me. Exposing what is in our own hearts often gives others the opportunity to open up theirs, and perhaps to even speak about something they have never shared with another soul.

Those who have been widowed have spoken to me of their great loss; those who have been betrayed have bravely exposed their hurt; those whose health has been snatched away by disease have shared their daily struggle to live. I have wept with parents who have buried precious children, and embraced those who have been denied the privilege of birthing children of their own. With each one I have tried to show them the love of Christ, sharing the gospel message of a Saviour who is our burden-bearer – from sin and through sorrow.

I doubt whether I could have done that as effectively if I had not stood where they stand – if I had not myself travelled the road of pain. Yet the sharing of what God has done, and continues to do, in our lives does not need a public platform. That can be just as easily accomplished in a more private fashion, as we get to know people one by one in our daily experience of life. Often it is the "ministry of presence" that witnesses – being there at the time when we are needed. A listening ear can be a great gift to someone who simply wants to mention the name of the one they've lost, one more time.

Wisdom in how we use our words is something we should constantly seek – even if we've gone through a similar situation, as no two people suffer in exactly the same way. Occasionally, people don't want to see the person who appears to have it all together while their own emotions still feel raw; so, when dealing with individuals, love is the first thing we should offer. Advice comes later ... sometimes much later.

For us, Cheryl's diagnosis threw us into a world whose existence we were aware of, but until that time, we had no idea how large that world really was. Over the years we met many amazing families who struggle every day to cope with disability and disease. They too have had their dreams destroyed, and plans devastated, when the child they had was not the child they expected. Every mother longs that the baby she carries in her womb will be well – few would even give a second thought to the possibility that it might not be. Even those who have a pre-natal diagnosis of abnormality always hope that maybe the doctor will be wrong – or that perhaps, things won't be as bad as they have been told. That "It'll never happen to me" mentality is engrained into our psyche.

Along with the parents we met were a multitude of brave and wonderful children. They constantly touched our lives as we watched them deal with situations that most adults could not endure.

These children are thought to live worthless lives, unable to make a contribution to the communities from which they come. Nothing could be further from the truth! I have watched God produce amazing results even from the lives of those who are seen as society's most unproductive citizens. They have been considered by some as a drain on society, both in terms of human resources and financial burden. And while they may be unable to add to the nation's Gross Domestic Product, or to bring a smile to the Chancellor's face, or to gain letters after their name, what they can do is worth more than all of that put together.

Their tenacity on life is remarkable – teaching us not to give up so easily. Their ability to smile at so little is humbling. These children are made of special stuff, challenging our complaining attitude to life, encouraging us to be thankful for all that we, the able-bodied, enjoy. And they have the remarkable ability to teach us to look beyond ourselves, when this world shouts out the message: "Look after Number One!"

God's ministering angels have had a remarkable effect on my life – they were people who learnt quickly to look beyond themselves to help care for us as a family. There were, however, some big surprises that came as a result of Cheryl's diagnosis. All types of personalities are represented in a large church, including those who find it easier to complain and moan than others. If it's cold they complain that the heating wasn't turned up; if it's hot then too few windows were opened; the music was too loud; the children too noisy. Wherever you find a group of people together – there will always be a complainer. I'm sure you know what I mean!

So it won't surprise you that the church we were attending at that time had a lady who fitted the bill perfectly. In fact, I couldn't remember a conversation with this lady that hadn't contained a complaint. She was hard work.

On one occasion Cheryl had only recently been discharged from hospital following a serious bout of pneumonia. It had been one of the many "she won't see morning" episodes that Cheryl had managed to survive. We were glad to have her back home with us once more. Cards with thoughtful messages were continuing to arrive, and so when the postman arrived I picked up the sealed envelopes to investigate their contents. A thoughtful greeting is such an encouragement.

One such envelope contained a beautifully hand-written note, and I must confess that I was shocked to see the name of the sender. It was from the lady who never had anything good to say – until this point. She began her letter by saying how very sorry she was to hear that Cheryl had been ill again: I was touched that she had taken time to write. Then she continued by saying how Cheryl had touched her life, listing thoughtfully how this was so. It was obviously written very carefully; each word measured so as not to cause offence, and chosen rather to deliver love and concern.

Before long the ink was smudged with my tears. I was so proud of my little girl. She may not have been able to walk or talk, or do anything that other children could – yet her life was powerfully impacting the lives of others. The lady finished her heart-rending letter by saying that Cheryl had helped her to take her eyes off herself, and think of others. What an admission! And all because of the bravery and uncomplaining spirit of one very sick little girl.

Yet, the pain of others should produce that kind of reaction from us, as individual members of the church of Jesus Christ. It should teach us to look beyond ourselves to the needs of others, and display itself in loving action.

Pain produces an occasion for the gospel in many different ways. Often it comes in the form of deeds of kindness, but it should also give us the opportunity to speak words of hope into the lives of the suffering. Those words of hope are not about woolly, wishful thinking, but about real assurance that can be found by faith in Jesus Christ.

Since Cheryl was only a few years old, I have been involved in ministry, mostly to women, to a greater or lesser degree depending on the health of my children at the time. Then after Joy died in 1999 the opportunities both to speak and write increased significantly. I am often asked to speak on the subject of suffering, and do so through Bible teaching and testimony. Very occasionally

I ask God if I should continue to do this – it's a long time to be speaking on the same subject! Each time I make my enquiry He always brings me back to the same verse of Scripture: "But I want you to know, brethren, that the things which happened to me have actually turned out for the furtherance of the gospel" (Philippians 1:12). Paul was telling the new believers at Philippi not to worry about his imprisonment – God was working out His own plans, both for him, and for the people he was in contact with every day.

"Your pain is not wasted, Catherine," God would say to my heart. *"Rather, the gospel will prosper because of it. So keep on going for now."*

God intends that what we go through will enable us to "comfort those who are in any trouble, with the comfort with which we ourselves are comforted by God" (2 Corinthians 1:4). This is not merely for us to see that something good is coming from our circumstances, but to afford us the privilege of bringing comfort to others.

That is certainly something the apostle Peter was able to do when he wrote his first letter to those of the Diaspora. Jewish believers had left Israel because of persecution and were now scattered across the Roman Empire. They had already suffered great loss when Peter wrote, telling them to expect further persecution ahead. The Roman Emperor Nero had become nervous about the talk from Christians about Christ's return some day to establish His kingdom. Because of this, Peter knew that severe, widespread persecution was inevitable, and he wrote to prepare the believers for what was coming and to show them how they should live in difficult times.

He encouraged them to concentrate on the end result of their pain when he wrote: "There is wonderful joy ahead, even though you must endure many trials for a little while" (1 Peter 1:6 NLT).

I wonder whether these Christians, who had already suffered for their faith, groaned when they read Peter's words. Or perhaps their earlier experiences had already developed within them the ability to trust God, no matter what life threw at them. They had already proved His sufficiency, but God, in His mercy, was sending them positive advice through this letter from Peter.

"These trials," Peter continues, "will show that your faith is genuine. It is being tested as fire tests and purifies gold – though your faith is far more precious than mere gold" (1 Peter 1:7 NLT).

How those words must have thrilled their hearts, as Peter reminded them of how precious they were to God. He explained that all they had already suffered because of their allegiance to Jesus Christ, and all that lay ahead, had a purpose. It would not only bring about refinement in their own lives, but would also a produce love and care for others.

"Most important of all, continue to show deep love for each other ... Cheerfully share your home with those who need a meal or a place to stay" (1 Peter 4:8–9 NLT).

Peter's letter is full of practical counsel, and is peppered with loving concern for his flock. He had personal knowledge of what suffering for Christ's sake was all about. Some of the recipients of this letter would have remembered only too well the beatings and imprisonment Peter himself had suffered from both the Jewish leaders and King Herod Agrippa. Undoubtedly some of them would have smiled as they recounted to younger family members the events of that day when they thought Peter would be executed for his faith.

They had been holding a prayer meeting in John Mark's family home. James, Zebedee's son, had recently been snatched away from the church and beheaded; and then Peter had been arrested. Those who met to pray for Peter knew that it was only a matter of time before Herod would also kill him. Their prayer was fervent and continuous, when suddenly the servant girl Rhoda burst into the room shouting that Peter was standing outside! They all thought she was mad and, in essence, didn't believe that God had answered their prayer. After all, Peter was chained to two soldiers in the innermost part of the prison, and just to be sure, Herod had commanded extra guards to be posted at the prison gates. There was no way Peter could be standing outside the door!

All present that day learnt a valuable lesson – if you are going to pray, you should believe that "with God nothing will be impossible" (Luke 1:37). For sure enough, Peter had been led safely out of the prison by an angel, and was waiting for someone to let him in!

As those now facing further persecution held this letter in their hands, they knew it did not come from someone who was unfamiliar with suffering. Its scribe was himself living proof of what God can do through one who has persevered when tested. Those of the Diaspora were reaping the results of Peter's suffering, not realizing that centuries later we would be reaping the results of theirs.

Down through the centuries evil dictators and violent governments have used persecution to try to kill off the church of Jesus Christ. In Soviet gulags, Cambodian killing fields, Chinese prisons, North Korean torture houses – by rape, pillage, starvation, deprivation and emotional blackmail – servants of the cross and simple followers of Jesus have suffered terribly, even to death.

The results have come at great cost, but they have come. Far from silencing the message of deliverance through faith in Jesus Christ, the persecution mushroomed the growth of the church in these places. Light has indeed shone brightly through the darkness. Apart from the huge part they play in building Christ's church today, brave, suffering members of the body of Christ can look forward to eternal rewards for their suffering.

"Instead, be very glad," Peter says, "for these trials make you partners with Christ in his suffering, so that you will have the wonderful joy of seeing his glory when it is revealed to all the world" (1 Peter 4:13 NLT).

We, too, are part of that same body, members of which are suffering today. Jesus commands us to "love one another as I have loved you" (John 15:12). His sacrificial love towards us is the example we are called to follow as we learn how to "bear one another's burdens" (Galatians 6:2). Our prayer and loving action can help to ease pain, bring comfort, and build the church in areas of the world where our brothers and sisters suffer the greatest.

When I stood in the dirt of the refugee camps on the Thai–Burma border I was humbled beyond belief as I recognized the privileges I have, and the depth of suffering it costs many to follow my Saviour.

Must I be carried to the skies
on flowery beds of ease,
while others fought to win the prize,
and sailed through bloody seas?

Since I must fight if I would reign,
increase my courage, Lord!
I'll bear the toil, endure the pain
supported by Thy word.

In the name, the precious name,
of Him who died for me,
through grace I'll win the promised crown,
whate'er my cross may be.

ISAAC WATTS[1]

Broken works best

"Look out! Bridge ahead, Dad!"

The Land Rover screeched to a halt, coming up a few feet short of the makeshift bridge. The word "bridge" was altogether too grand for the few rickety tree trunks that spanned the narrow river – without which it would have taken even longer to reach their destination. Jumping out of the vehicle to examine the latest obstacle, the children brushed up against the jungle vegetation, barely taking notice of the rustling noise as they did so. These were no ordinary children – they had grown up in the Congo and knew that most wild beasts ran off when humans appeared. But they were wise enough to keep a sharp eye on what was beneath their feet – snakes should always be treated with caution!

Now looking down into the big hole at either side of the bridge, Bob McAllister was glad that this was one bridge the rebels hadn't destroyed. If the Land Rover had tumbled over into the riverbed, it would have been more than just a nuisance; it could have rendered the vehicle damaged beyond repair. Unloading the supplies of food and clothing, along with the odd musical instrument, the children helped their parents carry the Land Rover's contents little by little across to the other side. The lighter the vehicle, the more chance the logs had of supporting its weight and allowing safe onward passage.

Alma started a little song as the job continued, her children joining in as they happily got on with what needed to be done. These forest paths had resounded with praise from this particular family before. The jungle tracks were now leading Bob and Alma, along with their three children, to the places they longed to be – places where they knew God had told them to go. A few blockages along the way weren't going to discourage them.

Since returning to Zaire (previously named Congo), the McAllisters lived for these treks away from the city. Based now in Kisangani, they relished the opportunity to visit their former mission stations and village locations deep in the Ituri Forest, even though permanent settlement there was not yet possible. As soon as the children returned on vacation from school the Land Rover was packed up, and off they went to see what had become of their wonderful Christian friends.

The treks always started with great excitement, accompanied by an amazing sense of privilege and joy. Yet this time there was an overwhelming sense of sadness at the frequent sights of devastation and enormous need that greeted them at each location.

It didn't take long to repack the Land Rover, although time was something that never meant anything in Africa anyway. As they sucked on juicy oranges after their work was done, a large parrot flew overhead, brightening the monotonous green of their surroundings. The village was now only a few kilometres away.

The road leading to their destination was very overgrown, so they made slow progress down its length. Bush grasses, thorny shrubs and overhanging branches made for a bumpy journey. It was obvious that little of any kind of traffic had passed this way for some time. As they approached their destination a sense of quietness replaced the happy chatter; prayer was offered from every heart in the crowded vehicle.

"Is there still a village here, Lord?" was the veteran missionary's fervent prayer. "Increase our courage, Lord – for whatever we find."

The Land Rover pulled into a large open space; a space that was once filled with simple tribal homes. On this occasion no children rushed towards them as they drove in; no broad, white smiles beamed back from black faces to welcome their arrival. The place was desolate – a sadness filling the very air. Jumping out on to the still-blackened earth, the family found it hard to speak. Alma looked in the direction of where the little medical outpost had once stood, while Bob momentarily dropped his head as he caught sight of a pile of ash. At one time it had been a church that was filled with the singing of many voices: filled with many of his dear Congolese brothers and sisters in Christ. It was the noise of his own children that drew Bob away from his heartbreaking thoughts.

His two teenage sons and his nine-year-old daughter were rattling around in the Land Rover, having begun to unload the vehicle. Each had been given a job to do. There were camp beds to erect and mosquito nets to string; a fire to light and food to be prepared. They knew that before long people would arrive, once they were convinced that it was safe to leave their forest hideouts. It was important to be ready for them – to give them the kind of welcome they had once afforded to this family from Ireland.

And come they did!

"Bwana Mackie!" came an excited call from the bush.

As Bob turned towards the sound of his name, tears filled his eyes to see men and women coming towards the village. Hugs and smiles rained down in abundance as Bob and Alma greeted their old friends once more. Some of the villagers were easily recognizable; others had been so maimed and injured by the violence meted out to them that the missionaries had to ask their names. Starvation had changed the shape of many bodies and added more age to faces than the years would have dictated. Living off what could be scavenged from the jungle, and the accompanying diseases brought by such a life, had taken its toll on these brave tribespeople.

"Mama Mackie," an emaciated little woman said, looking rather disappointed that the lady missionary didn't seem to know who she was. "Don't you recognize me, Mama?"

Alma looked closely into the bloated face of a dear woman who was clearly suffering from severe malnutrition. Her stick-like limbs and swollen belly were telltale signs of how ill she really was. In those few minutes Alma tried so hard to think who she could be, but without success.

"It's Marie, Mama – Marie. Don't you remember me?" In an instant, Alma remembered her dear friend. Standing in that one-time place of blessing, the missionary wrapped her arms around Marie, distressed that she had had to suffer so much.

Soon music filled the air, the trumpet blast chasing off the monkeys as it led the praise to God in a village that Satan had tried to destroy. The sound of Swahili rose in tuneful praise to the Lord, who had not abandoned His people as they fled from the Simba rebels. Sitting around the campfire, and at many campfires in the days to come, the McAllister family got to hear the stories of those who had survived those vicious months of rebellion. They also heard the stories of those who had not.

The rebels, indoctrinated by Chinese communist ideology, swept through the vast land of Congo, wreaking havoc in village after village. It was a case of "join us or die". Christians were tortured; hands tied behind their backs; kicked; beaten; ears were cut off!

"Renounce your faith and you will live," they were told. "There is no God!" the rebels would taunt as they inflicted pain.

Many were slaughtered, especially those who were known to have had any association with white people. Others escaped into the jungle – some with horrific injuries – all to face an extended period of deprivation. Then, before they moved on in their murderous intent, the rebels stole what they wanted, including the village livestock, and set fire to everything in sight. Not a stick was left.

Yet, those campfire encounters were far from only talk of sadness, as the African believers spoke of God's great enabling grace in the face of suffering. Their stand for God was unflinching because these people knew that it took great suffering for the Saviour to purchase their salvation. They knew what Paul was talking about in Philippians 3:10 when he taught the believers that knowing God involved "the fellowship of His sufferings" and "being conformed to His death". And the members of the Congolese church were able to testify that they had experienced the "power of His resurrection" in lives that, humanly speaking, should not have survived.

God was with them during the darkness of rebellion and the uncertainty of their nation's political turmoil. While thousands had been martyred, the missionaries were left in no doubt, as they listened to story after story, that the faith of those who had survived had proved genuine even though it had been "tested by fire" (1 Peter 1:7). They may have carried pain in their hearts and injuries to their limbs, but these followers of Jesus had come forth as gold. Their faithfulness was truly humbling.

Many were the tears shed during those campfire nights as Bob and Alma made contact once more with the people to whom God had asked them to bring the gospel many years earlier.

"Why did you come back, Bwana Mackie?" the people would ask. "It isn't safe here."

"I came back because the Lord told me to," he would humbly reply.

This identification with them in their pain was a true sign of the white missionaries' love for them – especially as they had brought their own children back into a country that was still far from stable. In addition, they knew that Bwana's and Mama's suffering during the rebellion was also great. UFM, the missionary organization they worked for, had lost thirteen adults and six children in the Simba Uprising of 1964. As Bob visited his African friends, they were a reminder to him of another friend who had made the ultimate sacrifice.

The Reverend Hector McMillan, a Canadian missionary, was known for being a great all-rounder. His practical skills were second to none, while he was also a man of the Bible and a great preacher.

As the school term had just finished, Hector, Bob and the other missionary parents had come to the Stanleyville headquarters of UFM to collect their children. It was customary that once the children had arrived back from the boarding schools, the missionaries would take them home to the remote forest locations where they worked.

Missionary service always involved an element of sacrifice, and so seeing their children again after weeks of separation resulted in much excitement. But the rambling old colonial house that served as UFM headquarters was buzzing more than usual that day. Each of the missionaries arriving from various areas around the province of Oriental had stories of unrest and sporadic roadblocks set up by a new group of rebel forces. There were men and boys menacingly brandishing bush knives in the city, while guns were also beginning to appear on the streets. Talk of turning Zaire into a socialist republic was rife on the rumour mill: tension filled the air. Once the children had returned and supplies had been gathered, the missionary families were keen to leave the city and return to what they thought would be the relative peace of their rural villages.

Squeals of excited delight filled the air when the children spotted their families as the truck came to a rumbling halt inside the compound. With everyone talking at once, and trying to catch up with weeks of news in a few sentences, a sense of normality returned, at least for a short time. When eventually the children succumbed to exhaustion, the adults were free once more to talk: there was little sleep to be had that night for them. Ears were pressed to the radio for any useful information that was floating on the airwaves, while much prayer was offered for a safe onward journey the following day. However, circumstances were to refuse them the opportunity to return to their mission stations.

Not much of the next day had passed before the roaring of truck engines and the screeching of brakes filled the grounds of the compound. Filthy exhaust fumes belched from the old, poorly maintained trucks. A rag-tag troop of armed guerrilla soldiers jumped down from the vehicles shouting orders, rounding up the missionaries and their children, and forcing them outside into the open air.

The Simba Rebellion had begun!

From that day on, all whites were to be viewed as a danger to the new Socialist Republic of Congo. Plantation owners and government officials – and missionaries – were at great risk of danger and death from this untrained and ill-disciplined rebel army. The trapped missionaries had no choice but to do as they were told. And so began four months of house arrest and privation. With a rebel outpost a mere 500 metres from their compound, and rebels passing by their gates continually, they were effectively hemmed in. Stories reaching them of slaughter and torture convinced them not to make any attempt at escape.

However, Bob McAllister was very concerned for the villagers of Pontierville that he had left behind. He didn't want just to sit there and do nothing. The pioneering gospel work had only begun in the area, so with a deep sense of responsibility to the people, he tried on three separate occasions to escape house arrest and see for himself how the locals were coping. However, each attempt failed, and each failure brought guilt to the big Irishman's heart. When he asked the Lord to open the way for him to return to the forest mission station, God prevented his success. It wasn't long before he found out why that prayer remained unanswered to his satisfaction.

Every last white person in the Pontierville area had been summarily executed by the rebel forces, as were even more of the Congolese people who had refused to join the rebel army. It appeared that God still had work for Bob to do; therefore He couldn't allow him to make the treacherous journey at that time.

Life was difficult for the families under house arrest, but they were thankful for each other, knowing that many missionaries were experiencing even worse conditions in other parts of the troubled country. Whilst others were starving, they were receiving some food from a local UN man, who passed by on his way home from his enforced labour on the rebel vehicles. A convinced atheist, this man had avoided contact with the missionaries before the conflict, but was touched by their acts of kindness during this time of civil war. A chink formed in his hardened heart and eventually he came to see his need of a personal Saviour.

Soon after he trusted in Christ, this dear man was brutally hacked to death by the rebels. His devastated wife was left to bury his body parts in a shallow grave.

To avert boredom, Hector McMillan and Bob kept themselves busy with the repairs on the old building, if and when they had the tools to do so. Yet their missionary spirit never waned – these two men were more interested in people's souls than in DIY. Finding themselves separated on one occasion from the rest of the group – imprisoned, no less – they found the cramped conditions of their confinement the perfect environment for evangelism. After all, they had a captive audience!

Following the custom of Paul and Silas, Hector and Bob sang hymns in the tiny room; and when they studied the Bible together, their five fellow prisoners had no option but to listen in. Even a rebel guard joined them on a few occasions.

Desperate times have a tendency to soften hearts towards the things of God, as the two men found out before they were sent back to continue their imprisonment in the form of house arrest. People were more ready to listen to God's Word when there was a real possibility of facing death in the near future.

The days merged into weeks, the weeks into months – and the conflict and terror continued unabated. The rebel fighters discovered that they were no match for the highly disciplined mercenaries brought in by the government to aid the national army. Yet instead of surrender, the rebels' response was to retreat, killing hostages as they did so. After four months of captivity, Hector and Bob knew that – one way or another – the end was close for their group of nine women, two men and fourteen children. But they also knew that Christians in many countries were praying for their safe release.

So they waited … and prayed … and listened to the radio.

The BBC World Service told them all they needed to know – unfortunately it also told the rebels. The relief of Stanleyville was close!

"Men, we are beaten!" crackled the voice on the airwaves. "Flee to the forest! As you go, sharpen your blades and take off the head of every white man, woman and child!"

The broadcast from the rebel radio station stunned Hector and Bob, causing them to cry out to God as never before.

Early the following morning the children ate breakfast in silence. Outside the sun was barely brightening a sky that echoed with the drone of incoming aircraft. A multitude of silhouetted figures canopied by parachutes darkened what little light there was above Stanleyville.

Hector looked at Bob. Today would bring rescue or …

"Out! Out!"

Mayhem ensued. Two rebel soldiers had forced their way into the kitchen, pushing and shoving, scattering the tableware as they did so. Tin mugs bounced across the floor as the missionary families were forced outside onto the sand beneath the mango trees. Roughly pushed together into a long line, they faced a firing squad of angry, violent men. Then something miraculous happened.

There was absolute silence!

The children – from as young as eighteen months old, older brothers and sisters by their side – stood bravely in the dust, without so much as a cry or a whimper from their lips. Satan may have thought he had the upper hand, but it was the presence of God that was evident on that fearsome day, under a beautiful African sky.

The motley bunch of soldiers fumbled with their rifles, the glazed look in their eyes testament to the amount of drugs it took to make one brave. Once they had managed to raise their weaponry to shoulder height, the order from a teenage officer rang through the compound:

"Fire!" he commanded with venom.

Still the silence sent from Heaven persisted. No weeping, no pleading, nothing – just a dignified silence from the Christians.

The missionary families stood bewildered, a few feet from their executioners. But not a single sound came from either weapon or rebel for what seemed like an age. These men had become familiar with slaughter, but on that morning they did nothing – their guns remained unfired! Still holding the rifles menacingly high, they kept them trained on the innocent in this terrible war of their choosing – like a freeze-frame on a camera. The unthinkable didn't happen!

Instead, the stunned silence was broken by another gruff command, given by a mere child, who, it seemed, had been taught to hate quicker than he had been taught to walk. Ordered back inside, the women and children were manhandled up the steps into the house and crowded into the living-room. In the confusion no one had noticed that Hector and Bob still hadn't returned to the house. Then without warning, a lone rebel soldier emptied his automatic pistol around the packed room! Bullets ricocheted off every surface, as the women and children fell to the floor.

As they were being led towards the rebel jeeps, Hector and Bob heard the shooting. Crying out in horrified response, thinking their families had been slaughtered, the men turned back towards the house.

Hector McMillan, Bob's dear friend and colleague in the gospel, was the first to fall in a hail of bullets. His blood seeped into the soil of his adopted country – his only crime that of loving its people for Christ's sake. As Bob turned to help his friend, another burst of gunfire dropped him to the ground, grazing his forehead. With quick wit, the Irishman played dead, as the violent youngsters walked around their bodies, checking for any signs of life.

Meanwhile, the gunshots had been heard inside by all nine women and fourteen children. Two of Hector's sons had been wounded, but none of the company had perished in the random attempt on their lives.

Outside, the story was different …

By the time the rebels sped off to continue their evil deeds, Hector McMillan was dead. The pain in Bob's heart felt much greater than that in his wounded head. One of the hardest things that man of God ever had to do in his life was to help carry Hector's body back to his wife and six sons. Thankfully, it was a task he did not do alone. His dear wife Alma, and a Canadian missionary, Thelma Wild, had bravely risked their own lives by running outside to see if they could help the two wounded men. With the sound of gunfire ringing all around them, they discovered that there was nothing they could do for Hector: he had already been welcomed into Heaven. Close by, Bob lay in the dirt, grazed and shocked, but alive. For that they were grateful.

With gentle respect, those three pairs of arms lifted Hector's body into the house, and back to his devoted family.

A short time later another two jeeps rolled into the courtyard, the background sound of gunfire getting louder by the minute. Rescue was close at hand. They would soon be heading for safety, and eventually home.

A few years would pass before they were able to return to Congo, and Bob frequently saw the kind face of his friend Hector in his mind's eye. The rebellion hadn't delivered what its perpetrators had promised. It had only delivered madness, evil and a terrible loss of life.

However, unlikely as it might seem, Bob knew that this was far from being the whole truth. God had used what had been learned in the revival, two years prior to the rebellion, to enable what had been a weak Congolese church up until that time, to suffer heroically for their faith. One rebel commander had once boasted that they would stamp out the church of Jesus Christ, and destroy the Christians' sabbath.

How wrong he was!

Today there are more churches in Congo than at any other time in history – strong in evangelism and sound biblical teaching. "The blood of the martyrs is the seed of the church", wrote Tertullian (c. AD 160–220), and that's still true in our age.

All of Hector McMillan's sons returned to Africa and built a church in memory of their father. That church is a vibrant, living testimony as to how God transforms lives: former rebels not only attend, but are in positions of leadership. Hector would have been thrilled. Three of his sons returned to Congo as missionaries; one served in Papua New Guinea; one in France, and the last of the six is an active supporter of foreign mission.

Bob and Alma's own two sons are still involved in mission work in the continent of Africa.

Many rebel fighters subsequently asked for forgiveness from their Christian countrymen, and more importantly from God – and have received it from both.

Undoubtedly, there was great loss, but both white foreign missionaries and African Christians agree that the results of this painful period in their church history have proven that, in God's hands, broken works best!

Heaven – the ultimate gain

Standing to attention in the hallway were three pairs of wellington boots. The great big green pair seemed to take on a protective role beside the petite red ones that were almost resting against them. Next in line, the even smaller yellow ones shouted out "sunshine" on a dull, rainy day.

The owner of the green boots now lay motionless at my feet. He would never wear those boots again! The stifled cries of his young wife at the end of the hall tore at our hearts, as she tried not to waken those who loved splashing in the puddles in those red and yellow boots. Both of us on the cardiac ambulance team that night had worked furiously, trying to save the life of a young father who was around the same age as ourselves. We were tragically unsuccessful.

Now, the much-too-young widow took me by the hand and led me upstairs. In a princess-style bedroom, filled with pink and frilly things, two tousle-headed little girls were fast asleep – each snuggled up with a soft teddy bear, each totally unaware of the nightmare that would not come with the night on this occasion, but would be waiting for them when they awoke. Feeling their lovely mummy begin to crumble in my arms, I quickly guided her out of the room, closing the door behind me. The morning would be soon enough to break their very young hearts. Death always breaks hearts.

Multitudes of authors have tried to describe its enormity by referring to death as the destroyer, the cheat, the thief, the invader, and the enemy. No description, however, is ever adequate to describe the part of life that brings the most pain: that time when the earthly person we are leaves behind those we love. For some, the actual event is worsened by its means: violence and hatred ending in murder; torture ending in martyrdom; carelessness ending in accident; sudden illness ending in unexpected parting; despair of life ending in suicide. For others, the edges of death's accompanying pain are temporarily softened by the knowledge that a long period of suffering or deeply difficult circumstances has come to an end. Conversely, for many, life's journey is simply over; age eventually overtaking the limited workings of the human frame.

Whatever the means, death brings with it not only sadness and separation; it also brings change. Life will never be the same again for those who have been left behind. The family or group dynamic that goes into making us who we are has been irreparably altered. Even those among us who love solitude can feel bereft when a significant person dies, because each of us has been created with the need for human companionship and interaction. Other people are important – and necessary – to us. Consequently, their loss can have a big impact on our lives, changing our secure environment into one that is suddenly more fragile.

That negative impact – sadness, separation, change – encourages the widespread response of treating death as the great taboo. We know it will bring pain; so if possible, we avoid talking about it – or even thinking about it. That suits Satan, the enemy of our souls: we think that if we don't talk about death we don't need to prepare for it. Somehow, even mentioning death transforms us into merchants of doom and gloom, in spite of what we Christians know about what happens to us after death forces itself to the top of the agenda.

Nevertheless, whatever we know about the future life from Scripture, we must never treat the death of someone light-heartedly. When Jesus arrived in Bethany after Lazarus had died, He wept at the loss of His dear friend, and for the sorrow of Lazarus' family – even though He knew He was going to raise Lazarus back to life (John 11:28–44). This amazing event gives us a picture of how Jesus deals with death. He is indeed the Master over what the apostle Paul calls "the last enemy" (1 Corinthians 15:26).

When he wrote those words, Paul was explaining to the Corinthian believers how vital the resurrection is to our faith as Christians: "if Christ has not been raised, then your faith is useless and you are still guilty of your sins" (1 Corinthians 15:17 NLT). In verses 21–23 Paul went on to explain that one man's (Adam's) sin brought about death for mankind in the first place, and that only through one Man (Christ) can the resurrection from the dead come. We die because we are sinners – we were born that way. The new life we obtain when we trust in Christ alone for our salvation means that when Christ comes back, all His people "will be raised" (1 Corinthians 15:23 NLT).

On that day, when Christ returns, we will be set free from the consequences of original sin forever. The final forces of darkness and evil will be eternally defeated, including the last enemy – death!

Even with this knowledge available to us as Christians, we frequently continue to look on death as the final frontier, the last place we as humans must conquer. Yet it is within our power to neither conquer it nor avoid it – it is a frontier to be crossed by every single one of us. Used in a different context, the word "frontier" is the most beautiful and accurate of all the descriptions given to death, because "frontier" simply means a border – the crossing-place separating two adjacent "countries".

The final battle may be pain, but crossing the frontier takes us from this country, Earth, to a far better one – Heaven.

Down through the years we have talked a lot about Heaven in our home. While such conversation has tinged our hearts with the sadness associated with the only means available to reach that place at the moment – death – it has also filled us with delight, joy and peace. And a few laughs along the way!

"Mummy, will Cheryl be able to eat potato crisps in Heaven?"

Our five-year-old son was only beginning to learn about Heaven. The time for the airy-fairy stuff was over. Paul needed to know that Heaven was a real place where his "big" sister, Cheryl, was going to go – probably soon, if the doctor was to be believed. And so began a steep learning curve for all of us.

I thought I already knew a lot about that place where the people of God will spend eternity. How wrong I was. In fact, I was to discover that I knew very little, and Paul kept our feet on the ground as we searched the Scriptures to learn more. As you will realize, once you mention a particular subject to a child at such an inquisitive age, he will talk about it incessantly. At first we found it difficult to talk to Paul about the fact that his sister, whom he loved dearly, was going to die.

"When will Cheryl die, Mummy?"

We didn't know, and as it turned out we would have her with us for several years longer than we expected.

What was very special, though, was that Paul chose to concentrate on where she was going and not on the fact that she had to leave us in order to get there. We did not hide the difficult facts from him, but perhaps it was easier to think about the fun things, rather than about the sad ones. I don't know; I only know that from that time onwards the subjects of death and Heaven have never been avoided in our home. Although the important issues to Paul were less than theological, we were reassured that in his young mind he was thinking things through.

"Will Cheryl be able to ride a bike in Heaven, Mummy?" he asked one day, almost knocking the double-buggy flying as he brought his bicycle to a screeching stop right in front of us.

"I don't know, Paul," I replied, frowning at his dangerous move, "but Heaven is a happy place, so she will have fun." "I'm sure there'll be bikes in Heaven!" he retorted, cycling on ahead of us.

At least he had grasped the truth that Cheryl's body would be transformed when she reached Heaven – because she definitely couldn't ride a bike here.

Heaven – the place of ultimate gain!

Heaven – the place where "Death is swallowed up in victory" (1 Corinthians 15:54), where the grave has lost its sting, where our perishable earthly bodies will be transformed into heavenly bodies that will never die. Our little boy had got it right – in Heaven everything is changed.

It is unlikely that any of us will reach Heaven's frontier without experiencing some degree of pain or suffering. That's why John's vision in Revelation brings such peace as well as jaw-dropping wonder:

> *And I heard a loud voice from heaven saying,*
> *"Behold, the tabernacle of God is with men, and He*
> *will dwell with them, and they shall be His people.*
> *God Himself will be with them and be their God.*
> *And God will wipe away every tear from their eyes;*
> *there shall be no more death, nor sorrow, nor crying.*
> *There shall be no more pain, for the former things*
> *have passed away."*

Then He who sat on the throne said, "Behold, I
make all things new."

REVELATION 21:3–5

The old world and its evils will be "gone forever" (verse 4 NLT).

Wow! It makes me want to shout with joy!

Our pain will be forever turned into gain. Sin will be finished once and for all, and therefore, its consequences will never touch our lives again. No pain! No sickness! No death! No sorrow! Every tear that has ever been shed because of the heartache of human living will be gently wiped away by our Heavenly Father. It can be difficult for our minds to take in what Heaven will actually be like.

And that's not all! The home of God Himself will be with us. He will not merely live in our hearts by the Holy Spirit – He will live amongst us in a way that we have never known before. With the curse of Eden now broken, we will live with God as was originally intended in His great creative plan.

It's no wonder that the apostle Paul said in Philippians 1:21, "For to me, living means living for Christ, and dying is even better" (NLT). Knowing what lay ahead in Heaven posed a difficult dilemma for the great apostle. "I'm torn between two desires", he said. "I long to go and be with Christ, which would be far better for me. But for your sakes, it is better that I continue to live" (Philippians 1:23–24 NLT).

Paul, like us at times, longed for his suffering to end. The prospect of being with Christ, and distant from the evils of this old world, can exert great magnetism, but desiring Heaven does not in itself take us there. Death, that final frontier, is in God's hands alone. He knows the right time for us to cross the border – He sees the big picture in His eternal plan.

Paul's bedroom door creaked open as he made his early morning trot to the bathroom. I lay curled up in bed, my husband sitting on the edge beside me, as our precious son passed our room. A surge of panic rose in my broken heart, as hot tears once again stung my aching eyes. It had been the night we had dreaded; the night we had expected; the night we thought we were prepared for. The dark hours of that night had seen Cheryl cross the final frontier into the adjacent country. She was in Heaven for Christmas.

"Dad? Why have you got your clothes on?" questioned the bleary-eyed eight-year-old as he turned in through the open door.

Without answering, his dad pulled back the covers to let him snuggle in beside me.

He knew there was something wrong, but it was my words that broke the silence.

"Paul, you know how we told you that Cheryl was very sick?"

By the dim light of my bedside lamp, he saw a big tear course furiously down my puffy cheeks, but he waited, not saying a word, his little body beginning to stiffen in my arms.

"Well," I continued falteringly, "Cheryl died last night – in the ward – and she's gone to Heaven."

His eyes widened as the shock hit, his chin trembling as he pushed me away – turning his back on the bearer of such awful news. Silently, his dad stroked his hair as I rubbed his slender back.

"I'm sorry, son," was all I could manage.

"You didn't tell me she was going to die!" he shouted, trying to pull away from my caress.

"But, I did – we talked a lot about Cheryl dying and going to Heaven one day," I reasoned.

"But you didn't tell me she was going to die *last night!*" "We didn't know … we didn't know that it would be last night."

Paul's reply was inaudible as the floodgates opened and he wept for his precious sister. The three of us lay together in our big bed for what seemed like a long time, already missing the pretty blonde little girl who had swept into our lives, and left us much too soon.

"I need to get up, Mummy," Paul said suddenly. "I have to get ready for school."

"It's OK, son – you don't need to go to school today." "Oh yes, I do. I have to tell my friends that Cheryl has gone to Heaven."

Jesus spoke in Mark 10:15 about receiving the kingdom of God as a little child. It is the simplicity of child-like trust that He looks for in our response to Him. As Paul insisted on dressing for school that morning, I knew that Jesus would be smiling on this little boy. His sister had died and was now living in Heaven; the simplicity of that fact helped Paul get through the next few sad weeks.

I found simple child-like trust somewhat harder to follow through on.

Every day I travelled the six miles to the cemetery. I simply had to go. I had to be near her. The little body I had loved and cared for during the previous ten years was buried under the soil in a country graveyard – and I missed her desperately. The fact that Cheryl had a new body just wouldn't sink in. My arms were empty and aching for the "old" body that I knew so well. Sometimes Paul and Joy came with me to the cemetery. On one such occasion Paul spoke to me from the back seat of the car as we returned home. What he said was mature beyond his years, when he announced that he had something he needed to tell me.

"Mum," he began.

Looking at his face in the rear-view mirror, I wondered what was causing the look of consternation on his normally smiley face.

"Mum," he repeated tentatively, "I have something I want to tell you, but I don't want to make you sad."

His words and tone surprised me – I had no idea what was coming next.

"I have decided that I'm not going to be sad about Cheryl any more."

"Oh," I interrupted, "why is that?"

"Cheryl was always sick – and that wasn't nice for her. Now she lives in Heaven, and she isn't sick now – so I don't think I should be sad any more."

And the words of the Lord in Revelation 21:5 hit me between the eyes: "Behold, I make all things new."

Paul was right; Cheryl's life had become unbearable for her, and now she lived in perfection ... she would never have to suffer again. As I glanced backwards once more, I could see that such a profound statement had taken a lot out of our young son.

"That doesn't make me sad, Paul. You're right – Cheryl is in Heaven and will never be sick again. It will just take Mummy a bit longer not to be sad."

A huge sigh of relief filled the car as the little boy, who had already witnessed so much pain in his own life, picked up his book to read. He had learnt early in life that God can turn our pain into gain – of the heavenly kind.

When we take time to think about Heaven it is usually the future benefits that grab our attention: the life with God; the absence of suffering; the rewards for service and the thought that the Lord Jesus has actually gone on ahead to prepare a place for us (John 14:2). But what about the here and now? Is Heaven about more than "pie in the sky when you die"?

Don Carson, in his book *How Long, O Lord?*, challenges our thinking on how God uses suffering in our lives to help us take our eyes off this world, and to make us "homesick for heaven":

In fact, we begin to wonder if pain and sorrow in
this life is not used in God's providential hand to

make us homesick for heaven, to detach us from
this world, to prepare us for heaven, to draw our
attention to Himself and away from the world of
merely physical things. In short, we begin to look at
all of life's experiences, good and ill, from the vantage
of the End.[2]

Heaven is "the vantage of the End" of which Carson speaks. What lies in the future should influence how we see what is happening today. It certainly did for those heroes of the faith mentioned in Hebrews chapter 11:

All these people died still believing what God had
promised them. They did not receive what was
promised, but they saw it all from a distance and
welcomed it. They agreed that they were foreigners
and nomads here on earth. Obviously people who
say such things are looking forward to a country they
can call their own ... they were looking for a better
place, a heavenly homeland. That is why God is not
ashamed to be called their God, for he has prepared a city for them.
HEBREWS 11:13–16 NLT

I wonder what would happen if we really understood that this world is merely our temporary dwelling place, and that Heaven is our permanent home. Perhaps we wouldn't hold so tightly to the things of this world – or fear our own call to the final frontier. We might even find it easier to believe that our present suffering "is nothing compared to the glory he will reveal to us later" (Romans 8:18 NLT). Pain gives us more than an eternal perspective; it reminds us of the certainty of eternal gain – Heaven. The thought of Heaven then helps to shift our focus from our pain to the Lord

Himself, and the place He has prepared for us. With Heaven in our sights, suffering loses its futility and becomes the purposeful path to God's great promise: "I will come again and receive you to Myself; that where I am, there you may be also" (John 14:3).

After Cheryl died, I stayed in the valley of the shadow of death (Psalm 23) for too long. Feeling that my grief was all I had left of her, I had wrapped it tightly around me, unwilling to allow the promise of Heaven to bring me any peace. It required a deep work of God to move me on and bring me to the place of perfect acceptance. When the time came for Joy to leave us almost ten years later, my focus was firmly fixed on Heaven. I had finally learnt to look at life's experiences from "the vantage of the End", as Don Carson would have put it.

Joy's last few years with us really were miserable for her. It was heartbreaking to watch her suffer, as her quality of life diminished. She had started out in life as our "wriggly, giggly Joy", but smiles were a rarity towards the end, as she bravely faced each difficult day. So when things were especially tough I would sing to her of Heaven, and whisper that soon she would be free from her pain. I would tell her of Jesus, and how He would be waiting to welcome her, and remind her that in a little time we would follow – joining both her and her sister one day.

Joy died at home. Philip, Paul and I took her in our arms to the final frontier, where we left her with Jesus. Our hearts were broken for our loss, but thrilled at the thought of Joy's gain.

Three days later our family joined together with hundreds of friends to say our final farewell to our darling little girl. Her daddy's glowing tribute to his precious daughter spoke of how she, in her weakness, had touched many lives, proving that broken works best in God's hands. As the small white coffin left the church, my eyes were fixed on the butterfly wreath placed on top. The wildflower wings moved in the spring breeze, reminding me that Joy was not a lifeless corpse in a white wooden box. She had already been transformed – made new! Her last enemy had now been defeated. Death could neither harm nor hold her. At that moment, years of pain were being replaced by God's ultimate gain. Heaven was hers to enjoy!

And for we who remain …

If God is for us, who can be against us? … Yet in all these things we are more than conquerors through Him who loved us. For I am persuaded that neither death nor life, nor angels nor principalities nor powers, nor things present nor things to come, nor height nor depth, nor any other created thing, shall be able to separate us from the love of God which is in Christ Jesus our Lord.

ROMANS 8:31, 37–39

Notes
1. Isaac Watts (1674–1748), "In the Name".
2. D. A. Carson, *How Long, O Lord?*, Inter-Varsity Press, 2006, p. 116.

Taking a closer look

- Examine 2 Corinthians 4:16–18 for yourself. Allow these words to help you to see your struggles through the lens of eternity.

- What can we learn from 2 Corinthians 1:3–7?

- Read a magazine or Christian periodical that contains articles about the "suffering church". Ask God to help you respond to what you read.

- Carefully consider the raising of Lazarus in John 11:28–44. What can we learn from this passage about how Jesus deals with the last enemy – death?

- If you have not as yet made the spiritual preparation necessary for the final frontier, then why not do so now? God's plan of salvation can be found in the "Romans route": Romans 3:23; 6:23; 5:8; 10:13; 10:9; 14:9.

- Look up the word "heaven" in a concordance – and enjoy what you read!

A note from the author

Finishing a book fills you with all kinds of emotion. Sheer relief at finally getting the job done and meeting the deadline precedes the childish excitement of that "school's out for summer" feeling! An overwhelming sense of freedom after the early mornings and late nights and thousands of words (and that's only the ones you have deleted!) makes you want to dance around the room. It's the inner shout of a satisfied "Yes!", knowing that all of the checking and tweaking is finally over – you can do no more.

That is, until the first little niggling doubt creeps in and you begin to wonder … have I done enough? Will the publisher like it? Will the readers love it, or, perish the thought, hate it? Is there anything I've written that could hurt – or disappoint? Will the theologians think my writing is too weak – or will the ordinary person in the street think it's too deep?

Before long you begin to feel slightly nauseous from the topsy-turvy effect of the scary beast that is your "finished manuscript".

Having run downstairs squeaking with delight to announce to my ever-patient husband that *Broken Works Best* was finally complete, I returned to my study feeling elated – or perhaps I mean deflated. The doubts seem to be perched on the top stair, ready to cut back my short-lived joy. Little questions were starting to form as I opened my laptop – this time to check my neglected Facebook page.

A message was waiting from an unknown visitor.

It was from a young woman, but what she could not know was that her words were being used by God to let me know that my writing was not about people liking or hating it; or even about being accepted or rejected as an author. The task He had given me to do was all about people who were hurting and what He could do with their lives. It wasn't about me – it was about Him. It was about how He alone could turn pain into gain.

In a few simple, short sentences the young woman told me that her little girl had died three years ago. She just wanted to thank me for how my previous books had helped her through those difficult years.

I felt her pain. Christmas had barely passed, and I knew she would be missing her darling daughter – just as I missed both of mine.

And I was humbled.

Humbled that in some way God had allowed me to be a small part of the big picture in her life. So I sat for a few quiet moments praying, bringing her to God – and thanking Him for putting the finished manuscript into perspective.

And I handed back into His keeping the words He had enabled me to write. My desire is that one day they might help some other mother, or father, or whoever, to discover that they are loved by a God who will never waste their pain.

This book has been a mammoth task, as I have tried to blend simple biblical teaching with personal lessons, whilst adding stories of individuals who have seen God turn their pain into gain. As with *God Knows Your Name*, I have included Bible stories, researching each one carefully to ensure accuracy. While *Broken Works Best* contains some elements of my own story, it is not intended to be autobiographical, but I have found that the sharing of God's dealings with us spiritually can be helpful to others.

A note from the author

I am extremely grateful to three people in particular for allowing me to share their stories in this book. I know that those particular chapters will have blessed your heart as much as they have blessed mine.

To Gordon Stewart of AsiaLink I say a big thank you for sharing the story of Nanda with me. I was deeply moved to discover that this young woman has not only suffered deeply already, but is prepared to choose suffering in the future, in order that she can follow Jesus in the strict Islamic culture where she lives.

How can I ever thank Andy Cardy for opening his heart to us and showing us what God can do with the deeply wounded? Andy was willing to be interviewed at a very difficult time for his family – between the verdict and sentencing of the murderer of his daughter Jennifer. For that I am especially grateful. It was deeply humbling to see such grace at close quarters.

And to dear Bob McAllister – a spiritual giant of a man – who touched more than the Congo for the Saviour. Thank you for helping to fire my own life with a burden for the lost. May God continue to give you souls until the day He calls you to Himself, when you will also be reunited with your dear Alma.

The book you hold in your hands would not have read so smoothly without the help afforded me by others.

To my lovely husband, Philip, I say a big thank you, not only for your encouragement and proofreading, but also for the use of your study! Being married to a minister has it uses – not least being able to consult the many commentaries found on his bookshelves. Their knowledge has helped keep me on the right track.

To my dear friend and proofreader, Liz Young, I apologize for making the same grammatical errors again and again. I'm sure you are glad that I was never a pupil of yours! Your understanding and meticulous observations are unbeatable. Bless you!

A big thank you goes to Jonathan Carswell and the team at

10ofThose for republishing *Broken Works Best*. Whilst I am grateful to Monarch for its initial launch, I believe this book has more encouragement to share with those who are suffering. This publication provides an opportunity to do just that. Thank you.

But it is to God alone I bring my praise. For over thirty years He has been turning my pain into gain, which is why I dedicate this book to Him. Take it, Lord, and do with it what You will!

Contact Catherine Campbell at:
Email: catherine-campbell@hotmail.co.uk
Website: www.catherine-campbell.com
Or connect with her on Facebook:
www.facebook.com/catherinecampbellauthor

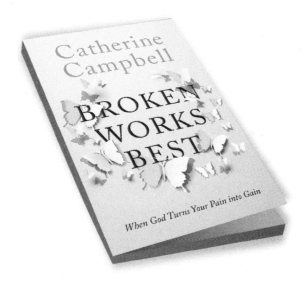

Publishing

a division of 10ofthose.com

10Publishing is the publishing house of **10ofThose**. It is committed to producing quality Christian resources that are biblical and accessible.

www.10ofthose.com is our online retail arm selling thousands of quality books at discounted prices.

For information contact: **info@10ofthose.com** or check out our website: **www.10ofthose.com**